ENGLISH 101

Guidebook & Reader

Eighth Edition

ENGLISH 101 FACULTY

Editors

Thomas Sura
Undergraduate Writing Coordinator

Sarah Morris
Associate Undergraduate Writing Coordinator

West Virginia University
Department of English

macmillan learning
curriculum solutions

Macmillan Learning Curriculum Solutions
14903 Pilot Drive
Plymouth, MI 48170
www.macmillanlearning.com

Sura 9750-3 F18

macmillan learning
curriculum solutions

Sustainability
Hayden-McNeil's standard paper stock uses a minimum of 30% post-consumer waste. We offer higher % options by request, including a 100% recycled stock. Additionally, Hayden-McNeil Custom Digital provides authors with the opportunity to convert print products to a digital format. Hayden-McNeil is part of a larger sustainability initiative through Macmillan Learning. Visit http://sustainability.macmillan.com to learn more.

bedford/st. martin's • hayden-mcneil
w.h. freeman • worth publishers

TABLE OF CONTENTS

ACKNOWLEDGMENTS

The selections written by WVU faculty and students are copyrighted by the respective authors and are published with their permission.

Thank you to the Undergraduate Writing Program Committee and the English 101 faculty at WVU for their excellent contributions. Special acknowledgments are extended to the following:

Sarah Morris

Laura Brady

Emma DiPasquale

Meredith Jeffers

Katelynn Lawrence Vogelpohl

Kelly Diamond

> Successful writers are not the ones who write the best sentences. They are the ones who keep writing. They are the ones who discover what is most important and strangest and most pleasurable in themselves, and keep believing in the value of their work, despite the difficulties.
> —BONNIE FRIEDMAN, *WRITING PAST DARK*

SOCIAL JUSTICE

The West Virginia University community is committed to creating and fostering a positive learning and working environment based on open communication, mutual respect, and inclusion.

If you are a person with a disability and anticipate needing any type of accommodation in order to participate in this class, please advise your instructor and make appropriate arrangements with the Office of Accessibility Services (304-293-6700). For more information on West Virginia University's Diversity, Equity, and Inclusion initiatives, please see http://diversity.sandbox.wvu.edu/ddei.

PREFACE

In her essay, "Composition as a Write of Passage," Dr. Nathalie Singh-Corcoran, Coordinator of the Eberly Writing Studio at WVU, writes that "the overarching goal of first-year composition (FYC) is to familiarize you with academic discourse (i.e., college level reading and writing) so that you can apply what you learn in future writing situations" (24).

She adds that, "while the goal is sound, you might be feeling a disconnect between the writing you are doing in FYC and the writing you believe you will do in your major and career" (24).

If that's the way you feel about English 101 at this moment then you're not alone. Each semester students enroll in English 101 eager to take classes in their majors or eager to figure out what those majors will be. There's often a strong desire to get introductory or general education courses "out of the way" in order to focus on bigger things.

Our goal in English 101 is to help you change that "disconnection" into a "connection." Throughout your course and throughout this textbook, we want to introduce you to the concepts, processes, and people—like Dr. Singh-Corcoran and your 101 instructor—who can not only help you advance to your major but also help you know what to do when you get there.

As you make your way through the different chapters and writing projects in this book, we encourage you to keep asking yourself how these ideas might apply to your major, to your future career, or even to your life. Think about how ideas of credibility in writing connect to ideas of credibility in your community. Consider how developing a process for writing connects to professional processes in the workplace. Reflect on how in-depth analysis of a text connects to diagnosing problems and finding solutions. Keep asking how and keep asking why.

By working with your classmates and instructor to see these connections, you will become a better writer and a better thinker. You will also be prepared for the more advanced courses at WVU, and you can meet the challenges they present with confidence. Ultimately, too, once you become really good at seeing connections, you will be better equipped to keep seeing new connections—between your academic life, your public life, your professional life, and your personal life. And when you can see how different pieces fit together, you also have tremendous power to reconfigure and reshape those pieces into new things, transforming the world around you.

We think English 101 helps set all of these things into motion, and we're excited to help you get started.

POLICIES AND PROCEDURES

Portfolio Grades (70%). *To be eligible for full credit, each writer must meet all major deadlines throughout the semester. The final portfolio must show evidence of the writer's process by including the required reflective writing and at least one draft version of each and every major assignment in addition to the final portfolio versions. Your final portfolio grade will be based on the following criteria:*

> All students will submit a final portfolio worth 70% of their final grade. Each portfolio will be 20+ pages, not including Works Cited, and will include reflection as well as evidence that the writer has met the English 101 learning goals. The reflective elements—whether an introductory memo, letter, or essay, prefaces to each entry, or in other forms—should address the assessment situation directly and identify choices the writer has made in including an entry or in preparing it for the assessment situation. Each part of the portfolio is expected to demonstrate the writer's care and competence in writing and rhetorical decision-making. If any of the components listed below are not passing, then the portfolio fails.

REFLECTIVE THINKING/ELEMENTS

EXCELLENT OR NEARLY SO	SOLID	COMPETENT	BARELY PASSING
4	3	2	1
Reflective elements positioned at the beginning or throughout the portfolio are well-developed and demonstrate the writer's insights and thoughtfulness about his or her learning in this course. The writer clearly identifies and connects the learning goals that he or she has met to the writing. The writer details why entries were chosen and how they were revised for the portfolio. The writer smoothly integrates key terms and concepts from the course content and materials (e.g., PACT, rhetoric, writing process, conventions).	Reflective elements positioned at the beginning or throughout the portfolio are thorough and describe the writer's learning in the course through explicit connections to the course learning goals. The writer adequately addresses why entries were chosen and how they were revised for the portfolio. The writer identifies and integrates key terms and concepts from the course content and materials (e.g., PACT, rhetoric, writing process, conventions).	Reflective elements positioned at the beginning or throughout the portfolio identify student learning but may lack explicit connection to course learning goals. The writer adequately addresses why entries were chosen and/or how they were revised for the portfolio. The writer makes some effort to identify and integrate key terms and concepts from the course content and materials (e.g., PACT, rhetoric, writing process, conventions).	Reflective elements are present but may be sparse or underdeveloped. These elements may make only broad or tenuous claims about the writer's learning in the course. The writer addresses only briefly why entries were chosen or how they were revised for the portfolio.

ATTENTION TO THE RHETORICAL SITUATION (PURPOSE AND AUDIENCE)

EXCELLENT OR NEARLY SO	SOLID	COMPETENT	BARELY PASSING
4	3	2	1
The writer consistently makes apt decisions about the contents of the portfolio. Any supplemental documents clearly connect to student's rhetorical knowledge, understanding of inquiry, composing process, knowledge of conventions, and/or reflective learning. Within the texts themselves, the writing has a clear purpose (thesis) and adapts expertly to audience through style, tone, and genre. The writer also smoothly integrates key terms and concepts from the course content or materials (i.e., genre, audience, revision).	The writer generally makes apt decisions about the contents of the portfolio, though he or she may show some inconsistency. Supplemental documents connect to student's rhetorical knowledge, understanding of inquiry, composing process, knowledge of conventions, and/or reflective learning though some of those connections may remain implicit. Within the texts themselves, the writing addresses purpose and audience without need for further major revisions. The writer shows some understanding of key terms and concepts from the course content or materials.	The writer's portfolio includes only the minimum contents (i.e., the major projects and reflection). The texts themselves have a clear purpose (thesis), but they would benefit from further revisions to clarify or enhance the purpose and adapt to audience. The writer refers to terms and concepts from the course content or materials but does so with moderate success or understanding.	The writer's portfolio includes only the minimum contents (i.e., the major projects and reflection). The texts themselves are coherent but generally require significant revision to purpose, development, and audience. The writer shows some understanding of key terms and concepts from course content.

SOURCES AND EVIDENCE

EXCELLENT OR NEARLY SO	SOLID	COMPETENT	BARELY PASSING
4	3	2	1
The writer consistently demonstrates skillful use of high-quality, credible, and relevant sources (scholarly; well-vetted popular sources; library databases). The writer uses these sources in a variety of ways: as background and context for a topic; as exhibits that help illustrate or explain; as evidence that corroborates or refutes claims; or as a method for research and analysis. The reader has no questions about sources or documentation. The writer also possesses fluency with and demonstrates the ability to conduct primary research (e.g., using interviews for the profile).	The writer generally uses credible and relevant sources throughout the writing. The writer uses these sources in a variety of ways: as background and context for a topic; as exhibits that help illustrate or explain; as evidence that corroborates or refutes claims; or as a method for research and analysis. The reader has no questions about sources or documentation. The writer also possesses some fluency with the ability to conduct primary research (e.g., using interviews for the profile).	The writer generally uses credible and relevant sources throughout the writing though the credibility may not be of the highest quality (e.g., an abundance of popular or tertiary sources). The writer demonstrates limited ability to use sources in a variety of ways. For example, the writer may only use sources as evidence to support a claim or may occasionally replace his or her own claims with claims from sources. The writer demonstrates little to no fluency with conducting primary research. The reader may have some questions about sources or documentation.	The writer generally uses credible and relevant sources throughout the writing though the credibility of a few sources may be tenuous (e.g., a poorly vetted blog or news site). The writer demonstrates some, though limited, ability to use sources as evidence. The writer demonstrates no fluency with conducting primary research. The reader may have questions about sources or documentation.

CONVENTIONS AND CRAFT

EXCELLENT OR NEARLY SO	SOLID	COMPETENT	BARELY PASSING
4	3	2	1
The writer consistently adapts to appropriate genre conventions and/or challenges conventions in ways that enhance the writing. Research is well-documented and well-integrated. The writing consistently includes little or no errors in usage, grammar, syntax, punctuation, or mechanics—none that impede meaning.	The writer adapts to appropriate genre conventions and/or challenges conventions in ways that are supposed to enhance the writing though they may sometimes fall short. Research is well-documented and well-integrated. The writing may contain a few errors in usage, grammar, syntax, punctuation, or mechanics—none that impede meaning.	The writer adapts to appropriate genre conventions but typically does not challenge those conventions. Research is documented and integrated reasonably well. The writing may contain some errors in usage, grammar, syntax, punctuation, or mechanics, and they may, at times, impede meaning.	The writer inconsistently adapts to appropriate genre conventions but does demonstrate some ability to do so. Research is documented and integrated reasonably well. The writing may contain errors in usage, grammar, syntax, punctuation, or mechanics, and they may, at times, impede meaning. The writing, overall, remains coherent.

Writing Exercises

Writing exercises are a means for experimenting with genre, style, and process, as well as a means for thinking through responses to readings, writings, and class discussions. You'll be asked to write for a variety of purposes and in a variety of contexts—in class, asynchronous and synchronous communications (message boards, e-mail, and chat sessions), and at home—alone and in collaboration with others. Writing exercises may be 1 to 2 pages in length. You can expect to complete about 10 pages of this writing throughout the course.

Writing Exercises (20%). Your process writing grade will be based on the following criteria:

A	The writing is well-developed, original, and succeeds in mastering new techniques and knowledge. The writing shows risks that work.
B	The writing has been done with considerable care and attention. It is developed and detailed.
C	The writing is acceptable. The student needs to spend more time or thought on the assignment.
D	The writing is unacceptable. It may be unfinished, inappropriate to the assignment, or written in class.
F	The student did not turn in any writing. (Please note: Late assignments are unacceptable.)

Participation

This class employs active learning in order to have the greatest possible impact. That means that your attendance and active engagement in class are vital to the success of the course and your success. Participation includes showing up on time to class each day. It also means being prepared by bringing your textbooks and materials. Anything that inhibits your active participation or the active participation of your classmates can negatively affect your participation grade (e.g., texting, playing video games). Finally, participation includes meeting deadlines, bringing drafts for peer review, making thoughtful contributions to classroom discussions. You can expect participation to count for 10% of your overall course grade.

Participation Grade (10%). Your participation grade will be based on the following criteria:

A	**Superior participation** shows initiative and excellence in written and verbal work. You were always well-prepared and on time, and rarely if ever missed class. More than simply being present, you used writing, reading, and discussion as ways to study how you and others make choices about language and form, understand complex ideas, and connect with others. Reading and writing assignments were always completed with attention to detail. In workshop or conferences, suggestions to group members were tactful, thorough, specific, and often provided other student writers with a new perspective or insight.
B	**Strong participation** demonstrates active engagement in written and verbal work. You were always well-prepared and on time, and rarely missed class. You played a consistently active role in large and small group discussions even if your comments sometimes did not add new insights. Reading and writing assignments were completed with attention to detail, with only an occasional need for further development. In workshop or conferences, suggestions to group members were tactful, specific, and helpful.
C	**Satisfactory participation** demonstrates consistent written and verbal work that meets basic requirements. You made it to class prepared and on time, stayed focused on the day's work, and never exceeded the number of allowed absences. You met all deadlines for drafts of major assignments, reflective writing, and exploratory writing assignment. You contributed to small group workshops and large class discussions, but your written and verbal responses could often have benefited from more specific detail or more thoughtful development.
D	**Weak participation** demonstrates inconsistent written and verbal work. Some examples may include a pattern of being habitually late to class, missing more than the allowed number of classes, being unprepared for class, or being distracted during work (e.g., texting, surfing the Web, chatting on unrelated topics, etc.). Weak participation may also be characterized by infrequent or unproductive contributions to classroom discussions. Weak participation is also characterized by missing several writing deadlines. In workshops or conferences, suggestions to group members may have been missing, too brief and general to be of help, or too late to advance the discussion.
F	**Unacceptable participation** shows ineffectual written and verbal work. Some examples may include a pattern of being excessively late to class. Other examples may include missing most or all writing assignment deadlines and submitting work that fails to meet basic requirements. A pattern of being regularly unprepared made it impossible to contribute effectively to classroom discussions or small group workshops. In workshops or conferences, suggestions to group members may have been missing, too brief and general to be of help, disrespectful, or disruptive.

Conferences

In addition to your regular class meetings, the English 101 curriculum uses small-group and individual conferences to provide you with more direct instruction on your specific writing projects. During the semester, you can expect to meet for conferences with your instructor or with small groups of peers about three or four times. You can also expect that during a conference week, one regular class meeting will be cancelled in order to make room in the schedule for the conferences.

When you are meeting your instructor or peers for conferences, you should plan to bring the following:

- Any questions you have about the current project

- Your exploratory writing you have completed for the current project

- Any drafting you have completed for the current project

Absences

We know that personal situations and required university events may, on a rare occasion, make it impossible for you to be in class. Remember, however, that's why a few absences are allowed; please reserve absences for emergencies.

- Students in all sections may miss one week of class without penalty.

- Students who miss more than one week of class may be penalized up to one letter grade for each additional absence.

- Students who miss more than three weeks of class will be assigned a failing grade for the course.

Note: In summer sessions, one week of class is defined as two class periods.

All absences *(including excused absences)* incurred from the date you register for the course will count toward the total number allowed. You are responsible for making up any work you may miss when you are not in class, even if the absence is necessitated by illness or personal emergency. This make-up work may include further exploratory writing, online work, telephone or e-mail collaboration, conferencing or peer review, and so on.

Please note: If you fail to turn in make-up assignments in a timely manner or if the make-up assignments are of insufficient quality, your instructor has the right to count your work as late or unacceptable.

Responsibilities When Absent for Illness, Injury, or Personal Emergency. If you have a contagious illness (such as the flu), severe injury, or a critical personal problem, you must, of course, take care of yourself. You do, however, have an obligation to notify your instructor immediately and you must arrange to make up any missed work in a timely fashion.

Responsibilities When Absent for University Activities or Religious Observance. In the case of university activities and religious observance, you must notify the instructor in writing and *two weeks prior* to the date missed. You must arrange to complete all scheduled work.

Avoiding Extended Absences. If you know in advance that you will need to miss more than three consecutive class meetings, you should take the course in another term. It is much better for you as a writer and as a student to take the course during a semester when your schedule allows you to be present to do your best work.

Avoiding Habitual Lateness. Late arrivals disrupt the class. If some unusual circumstance makes you late on any given day, please be sure that you talk to your instructor after class. If you are habitually late to class your instructor has the ability to record that repeated pattern as an absence. Please check with your instructor for specific details about the consequences associated with repeated lateness.

Attending Conferences. As part of this course, you will typically meet with your instructor for a conference three or four times each semester. It is particularly important for you to attend and be prepared for those meetings. Each conference will typically count as a full class day for attendance purposes.

Late Work and Extenuating Circumstances

Late work is unacceptable and may affect your participation, exploratory writing, and portfolio writing grades.

If you are struggling with an assignment, if you are unexpectedly ill, or if you have some other personal emergency, contact your instructor immediately and you may be able to negotiate a special arrangement. Such arrangements are rare and require a formal, written request to your instructor that must include an explanation of the circumstances, documentation (if relevant), and a detailed plan for completing any late or missed work. Submitting a formal request does not automatically guarantee that the request will be granted.

Cheating/Plagiarism

The English 101 community assumes your honesty. Students are expected to be familiar with the sections on Academic Honesty in the University Student Conduct Code, Policy Bulletin 31, which is online at: http://studentlife.wvu.edu/studentconductcode.html.

In English 101, we also expect students to submit their own *original* work. When you recycle your own past work or submit the same paper in more than one class, you are self-plagiarizing.

If you are repeating the class, you must talk to your instructor about whether you may use a previous assignment as the basis for further revisions.

If you are using a similar assignment for more than one class, permission must be obtained from the instructors of both classes. Permission is neither automatic nor guaranteed. Failure to disclose non-original or dual-submission work may result in an automatic F.

If you have any questions about when and how to document sources, or any other question that will help you avoid unintentional plagiarism (including self-plagiarism), please talk to your instructor. Plagiarism and cheating are serious offenses. Clear cases will result in an "F" for the course and appropriate academic discipline.

Document Retention

For your own records, make a photocopy, a back-up electronic copy, or other appropriate documentation of each project before submitting the original for review or evaluation. Technological glitches will occur, and it is *your responsibility* to be prepared for them. Because you will be asked to reflect on your progress throughout the semester, be sure to save all essays and projects that you complete.

Eberly Writing Studio

The Eberly Writing Studio is a resource that can help support you in all aspects of the writing process. It is located in G02 Colson Hall (the lower level). This is a free resource. You can meet with a tutor to go over the goals of any assignment or to get help brainstorming, organizing, or revising. The feedback from tutors will always focus on each writer's needs and abilities. Call 304-293-5788 to schedule an appointment or stop by to see if a tutor is available. Their website is http://speakwrite.wvu.edu/writing-studio.

Writing Course Concerns

In the event that you have a concern about your class or your assignments, please talk to your instructor. Most conflicts or concerns are best resolved through direct communication between the instructor and student.

If you still have a concern after talking to your instructor, please see Brian Kiger in the main English office (100 Colson Hall) to get a Writing Course Concern form. This form asks you to identify the nature of your concern or complaint and suggest a resolution to the problem. This form helps the writing program administrators respond to student concerns in an organized and timely way. You can usually expect a response to your concern within two working days from the time it is received (and always within five working days).

Technology in the Classroom

Technology can often enhance class activities, but it can also be disruptive unless used responsibly. Please turn off your cell phones, put them out of sight, and refrain from texting in class. If the class is meeting in a computer classroom, please be sure you are using the computers only as instructed for that day's class session (and not for Facebook or to check e-mail, etc.). If you are ever using technology in a way that is distracting or unrelated to the work of the class, you will be asked to put away the device or log off the computer. If your instructor has to discuss appropriate technology use with you more than once, you may be asked to leave and you will be counted as absent for that day. If there is an unusual circumstance where you must leave your phone on, please speak to your instructor privately *before* class.

COMPUTER CLASSROOMS IN ENGLISH 101

As an English 101 student you can expect at least half of your classroom time to take place in a computer lab. On a practical level this means that you will regularly meet in a computer lab. We provide this computer lab time as part of your learning in English 101 because we want to make sure that every student has some access to digital technology, and we want to create opportunities to reflect not only on writing but also on how digital technology influences what and how we write.

As students in a computer classroom, there are a few things that we ask you pay particular attention to. We encourage you to reflect on these questions individually or discuss them as a class with your instructor:

- How can you avoid distraction and use only online resources that are relevant for class work?

- How do you normally take notes and how can you use the technology to help you?

- How can you maintain a positive ethos in the class through your participation and your comments in online forums?

- How can you ensure that your work is properly submitted in all digital contexts? What should you do if you have a "tech failure"?

- What file formats are acceptable for sharing your work with classmates or your instructor? What programs are you using to compose your work? Do you know how to convert your files to other formats?

- How can you back up your files in digital spaces to ensure that you don't lose assignments or projects and to ensure that you have access to them from any computer?

- How can you get help if you have questions about using digital tools like eCampus or Google Classroom?

WELLWVU
The Students' Center of Health

Health & Education Building
390 Birch Street
PO Box 6422
Morgantown, WV 26506-6422
Adjacent to the Student Rec Center

Carruth Center for Psychological & Psychiatric Services • 2nd Floor • 304-293-4431 • well.wvu.edu/ccpps
Drop-in hours: Monday-Friday, 8:15 a.m.-4:45 p.m. • Extended evening hours by appointment: Monday-Thursday

- Group, individual, and crisis counseling
- Psychiatric evaluation, consultation and medical management
- Student Assistance Program (SAP) for alcohol and drug counseling
- MindFit screening, testing and treatment for attentional and other learning difficulties
- Consultation to students, parents, faculty and staff for student-related concerns
- Outreach presentations to the University and local community on a variety of emotional health topics

Emergency and After Hours Care
If students are experiencing a crisis or psychological emergency, they can call the CCPPS office at **304-293-4431** to speak with a counselor 24 hours a day, 7 days a week.

If a student or someone they know is feeling suicidal, the hotlines below can also provide assistance:
> National Suicide Prevention Lifeline: 1-800-273-TALK (8255)
> Military Veterans Suicide Hotline: 1-800-273-TALK (Press 1)
> Trevor Project (LBGTQ): 1-866-4UTREVOR (1-866-488-7386)

How you can help a friend who is struggling: Kognito Interactive Training

Interact with student avatars in this online game.
Topics include:
- Techniques to talk to a friend you are concerned about
- How to recognize signs of distress
- What support services are available on your campus

Try it Today
- Go to: **https://www.kognitocampus.com/login/**
- Select "Create a New Account"
- Enter your information and use the proper enrollment key:
  > Students – **wvu833**
  > Staff & Faculty – **wvu664**
- Select a course and follow the on-screen instructions (30 minutes)

For more information visit: well.wvu.edu/helpwell

Office of Wellness & Health Promotion • 1st Floor • 304-293-5054 • well.wvu.edu/wellness

- liveWELL lifestyle educational series promotes positive wellbeing and academic performance decision making
- Academic offerings: Enhancing Wellbeing PE 293 N, Peer Education CHPR 260/261, and Yoga PE 203
- Open Yoga classes for students, faculty and staff
- HeartMath lab teaches students how to self-regulate their physiological stress response
- Farmers Market weekly in the Fall
- Sexual assault prevention, including the Green Dot bystander program
- leadWELL mentor program trains students to initiate health-related conversations with peers
- Student leadership opportunities: Student Wellness Ambassador Team (SWAT) members, RDVIC Peer Advocates, and leadWELL mentors
- Safe Communities Initiative: collaboration between Greater Morgantown and WVU to enhance safety and wellbeing

West Virginia University
DEPARTMENT OF ENGLISH

What can I do with an English Degree in Literary and Cultural Studies?

Anything!

Why? Because the study of literature is the perfect foundation for a career in which careful reading, precise thinking, and the ability to write clear, persuasive prose are valued.

Studying literature is rewarding for its own sake, but it's about so much more.

Graduates in English literary and cultural studies at West Virginia University have careers in journalism, finance, marketing, law, advertising, the health industry, and many other fields.

english.wvu.edu

" I use the skills that I learned in the English Department at WVU every day in my work as an environmental litigator. In college, we read the best in literature, discussed it together as a class, and critically analyzed the work in writing. Today my life is a (more scientific and less literary) version of the same routine. I read complex statutes and briefs, discuss them with colleagues, and substantively respond in writing. "

KATE LOYD, '00
Trial Attorney, U.S. Department of Justice
Environment and Natural Resources Division

" By far the most outstanding feature of the English Department is its professors. The professors are not only accomplished scholars: they are always enthusiastic in the classroom, are actively involved in the wider community, and perhaps most importantly, are eager to take on the role of mentor. I am so glad I majored in English literary studies at WVU, because the skills I gained and personal guidance I received have truly set me up for success. "

MADELINE VANDEVENDER, '14
Quality Control Analyst
Johnson Matthey Catalysts

Literary & Cultural Studies

Students in the English literature program at West Virginia University

- ✓ Enjoy small classes
- ✓ Become excellent writers
- ✓ Study with award-winning faculty
- ✓ Acquire the critical thinking, communication, and problem-solving skills that employers want
- ✓ Take a range of courses
  - American and British literature
  - Shakespeare
  - Modern and Victorian literature
  - Multiethnic literature
  - Poetry and Drama
  - World literature
  - Folk literature

To learn more about
the English major and minor,
visit the Advising Office

Colson 100 • 304-293-9740
http://english.wvu.edu/under/advising

Professional Writing & Editing
Undergraduate Concentration & Minor

Both the concentration and minor in Professional Writing & Editing (PWE) introduce students to the theory and practice of writing, editing, designing, and publishing print and digital text.

Undergraduate Courses

Writing Theory & Practice
Editing
Multimedia Writing
Business & Professional Writing
Technical Writing
Humanities Computing
PWE Internship

Professional Experience

Students concentrating in Professional Writing and Editing participate in an internship to gain real-world, professional experience. This PWE capstone course provides a venue for students to apply the skills and knowledge that they have acquired during their training as PWE majors. Students intern with local and regional businesses, non-profit organizations, government agencies, and centers and organizations within WVU.

"At its best, the sensation of writing is that of any unmerited grace. It is handed to you, but only if you look for it. You search, you break your heart, your back, your brain, and then—and only then—it is handed to you."
—Annie Dillard

"The excellency of every art is its intensity, capable of making all disagreeables evaporate."
—John Keats

"Odd how the creative power at once brings the whole universe to order."
—Virginia Woolf

"Perhaps the truth depends on a walk around the lake."
—Wallace Stevens

Creative writing workshops at WVU will help you find the vital stories growing within you and learn to craft them in your voice through creative nonfiction, fiction, and poetry.

CHAPTER 1

Writing Your Story in English 101

OVERVIEW OF ENGLISH 101

English 101 is an introductory writing course designed to help you learn about writing so that you can use it as a major tool for success in college and beyond. While each English 101 instructor may use his or her own unique approach to teach the course, there are some core characteristics that all sections of English 101 have in common.

Chapter 1 is all about helping you see those characteristics so that you're set up to be successful in your 101 course. This chapter covers the following topics:

- Writing portfolios and why you have to make one

- The arrangement of the book chapters

- The course goals

- What PACT means and how you will use it

> For even more on the purpose and goals of English 101, read "Composition as a Write of Passage" by Nathalie Singh-Corcoran.

English 101's Portfolio Approach

Writing is an ongoing process. To keep track of both your process and your progress over the course of the semester, you will collect all of your written work to create a portfolio of your writing. The portfolio emphasizes revision and encourages you to reflect on your work as a writer, reader, and thinker in English 101.

On the schedule of work due, you will see "final-for-now" deadlines for each of the four major projects in the course. Throughout the writing process, you will receive feedback from peers as well as your instructor.

All of the feedback you receive will help you make decisions about revision, editing, and proofreading your papers. There are two important things to know.

1. The feedback from your instructor will not include a letter grade.

Not receiving a grade on each paper will probably feel weird, but we do it for two reasons. First, we would rather evaluate your work based on what you've learned by the end of the course instead of evaluating your work while you're still practicing and learning. Second, we know from research and experience that students often stop writing once they receive a letter grade because a grade signals the end of the writing process. We want to give you the opportunity to keep working.

2. You will need to make decisions about your own work.

Writing can be a complex process. To get the most from this course, you need to take ownership of your work and make decisions about how to achieve your goals in writing. Your instructor will always be there to support and guide you, but your instructor cannot make those decisions for you. Therefore, you shouldn't expect your instructor's feedback to be a checklist for achieving an A. You must use all of your feedback to make decisions, apply all of your learning to all of your work, and demonstrate your knowledge of writing and rhetoric throughout your portfolio.

At mid-semester, you will be asked to create a mid-term portfolio. This is a practice attempt so that you can remedy any trouble spots before you hand in your final portfolio at the end of the term. This also gives your instructor an opportunity to provide you with an in-progress grade so that you have a realistic sense of where you stand in the course at the midpoint of the semester.

At the end of the semester, you will compile your final portfolio (See Chapter 7). The final portfolio is your chance to reflect on your work as a writer, reader, and thinker in English 101.

FOUR MAJOR PROJECTS AND PORTFOLIOS

Each English 101 course will ask students to complete four major projects that address four different purposes for writing. You will have the chance to develop each of your major projects through a process of getting started, shaping and drafting, reviewing and revising, and polishing and editing. You'll compose papers in and out of class, alone, and in groups. These major projects will be the main content of your course portfolio. In total, you can expect to write 20 or more pages for your four major projects. This writing will comprise the biggest chunk of your portfolio, which counts for 70% of your final grade in the course.

For some of your writing, your instructor may ask you to bring enough draft copies to share with your group or will ask you to e-mail your papers to group members for an online workshop.

COURSE GOALS FOR ENGLISH 101

The undergraduate writing program at West Virginia University has developed a set of four course goals that all of our instructors use to guide our teaching. These goals are based on the "Outcomes Statement for First-Year Composition" published by the Council of Writing Program Administrators.

Goal 1: Rhetoric—Identify and interpret communication situations, goals, and audiences

Goal 2: Inquiry—Explore and analyze ideas through reading and composing

Goal 3: Processes—Demonstrate processes for composing and research

Goal 4: Conventions—Recognize and use writing conventions appropriate for various contexts

Goal 1: Rhetoric—Identify and Interpret Rhetorical Situations

When writing teachers encourage you to understand the rhetorical situation of your writing, they are referring to factors such as purpose, audience, conventions, and trouble spots (i.e., PACT for short).

For example, when you write an e-mail to a friend you probably automatically run through this list without thinking much about it. You might use the e-mail's subject line to explain why you are writing. You might reference a joke or an experience you know your friend will understand. You might use conventions of informal writing like LOL or ICYMI to communicate an idea. You might even change a word or a phrase to avoid having your friend misinterpret you. These are all important elements of rhetorical situations.

By the end of 101, you should be able to:

- Identify and describe the important components of a rhetorical situation

- Focus on a purpose for writing and understand what form your writing should take depending on the rhetorical situation

- Apply your understanding of rhetoric to your choices as a writer

- Understand what it means to write for an "audience" and be able to express how different audiences might have different expectations for your writing

Goal 2: Inquiry

In the context of English 101, it is important for you to be able to use writing and reading as a way to explore, to analyze, and to reflect. Each of these activities involves inquiry—that is, examining and investigating the facts and principles that help you understand something.

By the end of 101, you should be able to:

- Examine your own writing abilities and progress

- Use writing to find answers to problems

- Do research through interviews and the web

- Select and use evidence from your research to support your purposes for writing

Goal 3: Processes

Writing is a process. That means it takes more than one step, and the steps may not happen in the same order every time.

Even writing a short e-mail in less than five minutes may involve processes like looking up information; writing sentences; editing sentences by using your mouse and the delete key; reading what you wrote to make sure it sounds right; and so on.

All of these processes happen before you press the send key. Sometimes you might even need to repeat steps to get your writing done. This course will help you identify the steps in your writing process, add valuable steps that can help you, and help you sort out when to do what and how to do it.

By the end of 101, you should be able to:

- Use flexible strategies for coming up with ideas for writing, drafting, revising, editing, and proofreading

- Collaborate with others to give and receive feedback on writing

- Identify what parts of the writing process work best for you as a writer

- Find and use technologies that help you communicate and do research

Goal 4: Conventions

When writers talk about conventions in writing, they simply mean "the way things are typically done." As a communicator, it is important that you know the underlying "rules" of writing.

One part of that knowledge comes from being aware of the traits that distinguish one type of writing from another (different types are called different **genres)**.

A second part is giving credit to others when you use their ideas and language to support your own ideas. Writers typically do that through things like in-text citations and Works Cited pages.

Finally, a third part of understanding conventions means being able to control things like punctuation and spelling. Because there are a lot of these rules to remember, it's also important that you're aware of what resources you have to use when you don't know the rules.

By the end of 101, you should be able to:

- Identify and write in different genres for different rhetorical situations
- Use appropriate conventions for different genres including integrating and documenting sources
- Use appropriate punctuation and spelling
- Use MLA citations for documenting work
- Use MLA conventions for formatting your paper

CHOOSING A TOPIC

One thing your instructor may ask or encourage you to do is choose a topic for the semester. You may be used to choosing a different topic for each paper you write, but there are several advantages to developing a single topic over the course of the semester.

The first advantage is focus. Choosing a single topic to focus all of your projects on means that you can build up your knowledge on that subject. It actually feels like you're getting somewhere instead of starting from scratch every three or four weeks.

The second advantage is that because you are building up your knowledge on one subject over the course of a semester, you become something of an expert on that topic or issue. *This is actually really important for understanding rhetoric.* As an expert, you have a more persuasive ethos—or credibility—on a subject than someone who is brand new to the conversation. Focusing on a topic and developing your knowledge on that subject give you a chance to feel like an expert.

How to Choose a Topic

While you have a lot of freedom and flexibility with the topic you choose, you should keep in mind that not all topics are equal. Some will be more fruitful than others. Here are a few simple steps to help you develop a strong academic topic for your English 101 course.

STEP 1: ASK YOURSELF WHAT YOU'RE INTERESTED IN LEARNING ABOUT, NOT WHAT YOU WANT TO PROVE.

This step is first because it's essential to Goal #2: Inquiry. You want to choose a topic that you're open to learning about—something that intrigues you. What questions do you want to find answers to?

One of the **trouble spots** that students sometimes face is when they choose a topic that they think they already know the answer to. They aren't interested in learning new things, only solidifying why they are right and others are wrong. This sort of approach won't help you much in English 101 because this context focuses on learning and growth, not cementing old ideas.

Can you think of topics or questions that might be appropriate for English 101? Try completing a few of these sentences:

I'm curious about…

I want to know why…

I've always wondered…

STEP 2: START MAKING A LIST OF QUESTIONS YOU NEED TO ANSWER TO BECOME AN EXPERT ON YOUR TOPIC.

Remember, you're not committed to anything yet if you don't want to be. The idea is just to give yourself some time and space to see what topic is most interesting to you.

One way to do this is to make a list of questions related to the topic you have in mind—just some basic questions to start building your expertise. Here's an example:

Julia is a student in the School of Natural Resources. She loves the outdoors, and she wrote down the following when she completed the previous step:

"I've always wondered about the National Parks. I went to one once, and I thought it was really cool."

Now Julia starts to think about what questions she would need to ask in order to build her expertise on the subject. She creates a list of questions that immediately spring to mind:

- *What are national parks?*

- *Where did they come from?*

- *How old are they?*

- *How many people do they employ?*

- *Why do we have national parks?*

- *How many people work for national parks?*

- *How could I talk to someone who works at one?*

- *Do they have internships?*

- *How many people go to national parks each year?*

- *Why do people go to parks?*

- *Why don't people go to national parks?*

- *I heard that national parks might be shrinking? Is that true? Why?*

Notice that in the last question Julia wrote down something she heard. She doesn't have to worry about whether or not it's true at the moment. That might be part of her research. Her only goal at this point is to think through what she might want to find out.

Now it's your turn. Choose one of the things you wrote about in step 1 and make a list of questions you might want to answer. Use the space below to write your questions.

NOTES

STEP 3: SHARE YOUR IDEA.

One very important part of academic writing is sharing it with others. Sharing your ideas with others—classmates, friends, family, teachers—allows you to gain new perspectives, information, and stories that help to create a more complete picture of a topic or issue.

By sharing your idea with someone else you can test whether or not it's a good fit for English 101. You might also hear a new perspective on the topic or hear a new question that you want to answer.

Try sharing your topic idea with your instructor or someone in class. Ask them what they think and if they have any other ideas about questions you could try to answer.

CONCLUSION

As you move into the next chapter, you'll want to make a decision about your focus for the course. Each project from here on out will ask you to look at your subject in a different way.

Remember you don't have to answer all of the questions you have. You may just answer one or two of them with each project, and you may even realize that you have even more questions that you're curious about. That's okay! That's what academic discovery is all about—finding new questions to explore.

CHAPTER 2
Telling Your Story

In this chapter, you will write in order to tell a story about something compelling to you; you will revise and polish that story to make it compelling to a reader, as well.

GETTING STARTED

Story is a part of culture and knowledge. People are enthralled and entertained by stories. They use stories to deepen their understanding of the world around them, to articulate their beliefs, and to connect to other people. Some theorists say that story is the doorway to the collective unconscious. Regardless of how you look at it, making a story is an act of making meaning.

Story can help people make decisions about what is important to them and to communicate those ideas to other people to establish common ground. This chapter asks you to tell a story that matters to you and that can ripple out to others, to show how the events, ideas, or inquiry inspired by the story can matter to them, too.

Purpose

The purpose of this assignment is to develop a cohesive and meaningful piece of narrative writing that illuminates for a reader an important moment or event; you will also practice important elements of writing like description, organization, analogy, and tension.

A typical genre for this type of work is the narrative. Your narrative is one of the primary projects that you will put into your portfolio. Narratives can be a way into understanding lived human experience. They demonstrate how people experience events and how they make sense of those events. In scholarly writing, narrative is used when writing case study, ethnography, and illustrative anecdote, and it is used across fields such as the sciences, humanities, education, and social sciences. See the end of this chapter for an example narrative, or spend some time with examples your instructor provides.

Audience

Your instructor may have specific instructions about what audience to write for. Otherwise, consider writing for an audience of people who will be interested in the kind of story you are telling. In other words, you might write for an audience of other 101 students who will benefit from understanding your experience—perhaps because it is familiar, or maybe because it's foreign.

Conventions

Narratives often follow a clear pattern of organization, developing a series of important events in vivid detail. They have a beginning, a middle, and an end. They "zoom in" on important parts of the story, slowing down, and then "zoom out" on less important parts. They play with time by speeding up and slowing down with description to create tension and flow. There are countless ways that authors organize and develop stories. Listen for your instructor to give you specific instructions and examples. Possibilities often include flashbacks, multiple genres, or even multiple perspectives.

Trouble Spots

Trouble spots are the things that most frequently prove to be obstacles for writers. Along with your instructor, you may identify other trouble spots you want to discuss, but here are a few that writers encounter regularly:

* How do I write about something that matters to me so that it matters to a reader, too?

* Which details are most important to develop? Which ones can I leave out?

* How do I develop dialogue between speakers in my story?

Take a moment to see if you can provide your own answers to these questions. Then take a minute to jot down your own questions that aren't on this list.

Assessment

Your instructor may adjust the criteria below to fit the specific project for your course. In any case, here are a few key criteria to keep in mind:

* This paper will use a narrative base (in other words, your writing sounds like a story).

* This paper will convey a personal experience in a way that is interesting and relevant to an audience and provides a basis for inquiry in the world.

* This paper will use descriptive detail and examples appropriate to your purpose(s) and audience(s).

* This paper will convey some source of tension in the story that eventually turns toward a resolution or a question in the world.

* This paper will reflect on the new perspective you have gained since the experience and how it ripples out beyond you as a narrator.

* This paper will be approximately 1,200 to 1,500 words (4–5 pages) of polished writing.

FREEWRITING

Freewriting is an activity meant to help you come up with ideas and record them. Despite how "free" it sounds, there are actually two important rules for freewriting that will help you get the most out of the activity:

1. **Do not worry about spelling, grammar, and punctuation.** That's right! Forget about all that stuff that slows you down, makes you worry your writing isn't good, or causes you to pause every 10 seconds and reread what you wrote. Just write. Focus on getting the ideas down on the page.

2. **Do not stop writing.** This is the part that gets people. Some writers have a tendency to stop writing when an idea or a sentence ends, and they're trying to think of what to write next. When you're freewriting, you want to fight this urge. Keep writing even if you have to write, "I don't know what to write next" five times. Keep going until a new idea pops out.

Ok, are you ready? Try a short freewrite for 3 minutes on this page. Here are some questions to help you:

- What is a significant topic, idea, or moment that changed or influences your understanding of the world and that others should know about?

- What's something that has happened to you that could allow your thinking to "ripple out" into thinking about how that experience could be different and the same for other people?

- What is a significant event that has affected you and that would resonate with an audience?

- What's a story that uncovers an issue that has affected you—and that others have written about and researched, too?

This can be something small, like the time you got your first "C" because you couldn't master cursive writing or catching your first fish, or something big, like adopting your dog from the shelter or the day you arrived in Brazil for your study abroad semester.

Ready. Set. Go.

_____

_____

_____

_____

_____

_____

_____

_____

NOTES

_____

_____

_____

_____

_____

_____

_____

_____

_____

_____

_____

_____

_____

_____

_____

_____

_____

_____

_____

_____

_____

How did it go? Freewriting can feel kind of awkward at first if you're not used to doing it. Just remember that freewriting is a great way to get some ideas flowing for a new project or for a paper you're stuck on—it can happen at any point during the writing process. It can be a useful tool. It's also an activity categorized as invention.

> In writing, invention is a term we use to talk about how we come up with new ideas.

The textbook will address invention even more in the chapters to come. You can also look in *Easy Writer*, "Section 2: Exploring, Planning, and Drafting" for more ideas.

Activity: Reading Like a Writer

While people often read for pleasure or to learn a new concept, one thing is for certain—reading is inherently linked to writing; you can't do one without the other. As students of writing, try to read like a writer and notice the techniques that other writers use. This can be especially helpful when you look to professional exemplar texts or student mentor texts as models from which to learn something about writing.

You can expect your instructor to offer some kind of examples for you to read and look closely at to learn about narrative writing as a genre. There is a mentor text in this book, but the more examples you read, the greater your sense of the writing will be. As you read, try to consider the list below.

- Look at the title of the work. What do you expect before you read? Once you have finished reading, take another look at the title. Is it effective? How do titles keep their readers in mind? Can you suggest an alternative title? What title will you give your own narrative? Try brainstorming a few ideas.

- How does the writer use detail, imagery, metaphor, structure, voice, style, point of view, verb tense, headings, dialogue, images, other documents, organization, plot? List a few specific techniques you admire in the text you are reading.

- Find a single passage that catches your attention in some way. How did the author achieve this effect? How did she/he make this technique work?

- As you read, look for one or two techniques that you admire or that you've never tried before. How might you take a similar risk in your own writing?

- Try revising a section of your narrative by using one of the techniques you've just listed. Be sure that you are borrowing the technique only (not the ideas!).

- If the writer has used more than one type of document (more than one genre), how are the other documents woven in? What helps the different pieces hang together? Have you considered adding images or other types of texts to your narrative? What will help your text hang together?

> **Suggested Reading**: To learn more about reading like a writer, check out Mike Bunn's essay "How to Read Like a Writer." The complete citation for the essay is on the *Work in Progress* Works Cited page.

ANNOTATING A TEXT

Have you ever read a magazine article or a textbook chapter for school, gotten to the end of it, and asked yourself, "What did I just read?" Or maybe you go to the library, pull out your highlighter, and then highlight every single word because it all seems so important. Reading, understanding, and remembering a piece of writing can be a tough job. Reading, understanding, and remembering a piece of writing can also help writers improve because it allows them to look closely at the techniques and moves the author makes to convey a message or evoke a feeling in us as readers.

To help with this, it is important to develop strategies for annotating a text.

> To annotate simply means that you "add notes or comments" to something ("Annotate").*

There is no one correct way to annotate a text, but you may find it helpful to have a system. Try some of the ideas below and see what works best for you.

When you read a narrative, you might:

- Use two different colored highlighters. Use one color to highlight the details that help you decipher the main point or argument of the piece and another to highlight the significant moments in the narrative that move the plot forward.

- Use a pen to underline the most important sentence in each paragraph.

- Write questions in the margin when you get confused or need more information.

- Place a star next to words, phrases, or excerpts that interest you as a writer—for style, structure, craft, or detail.

In other kinds of texts, you might look for claims, argument, and evidence; rhetorical strategies; use of sources; or other kinds of information.

Practice using these strategies on the examples in this text or on the examples provided by your instructor.

For more on reading critically and analyzing texts, see "Section 7: Analyzing and Reading Critically" in *Easy Writer*.

---

* Pssst! Down here. In the writing above, we quoted a definition from the *Merriam-Webster Dictionary*, and we included an in-text citation for it. This might be helpful if you ever quote a dictionary definition in your own work. Check the Works Cited section at the back of this book to see an example of how to cite a dictionary definition.

Activity: The Down Draft

Now that you have had a chance to think about narratives and consider some examples, it's time to get started on your own story. The following strategies can help you generate a quick draft that you can use as a starting point. Write quickly for ten minutes, without planning or organizing—but also without stopping! Write what you remember. If you get stuck, write "I'm stuck here" and go on. If you know what you need to do but can't do it yet, describe it. Try one or more of these activities and see where they lead you.

1. **Three moments.** Choose at least three distinctly separate time periods in your life. Begin each section with "I am _____ years old," and freewrite from there for ten minutes. (An alternative is to think of three songs or three photographs from distinctly separate times in your life. If you choose this option, start each section with a title or caption.) Stay in the present tense. After reading what you've written, see whether you can find any thematic connections or common images that would link the sections together. You might also consider what happened in the world, in history, during the time of these events and how that might tie into your own history.

2. **Three readers.** Focus on one event. Who would be interested in the event? Who might learn something from your story? Who might give you a new insight? One reader might be a stranger who witnessed the event; another might be a new friend who would understand something about you from your story; yet another might be a much younger or much older person (perhaps a young cousin or a grandparent); another might be a person in authority. No matter who you choose for your three readers, be sure they differ in terms of what each knows about you and what they need to know. Write for about three minutes as you tell the same story to each of the readers you have in mind.

    How much background information do you need to give each reader to make the most impact? What language, details, images, or genres change as you tell the story more than once to different types of readers? How might you connect these three accounts? What language, details, or images might recur in all three accounts? (An alternate approach might try three different genres to tell the same story such as a letter, a news release or news article, and a Facebook profile. Again, the challenge is to consider what changes, what stays the same, and what connects the three.)

3. **Flashdraft.** Choose one important life event that has had an impact on your present view of life in general—it might be something you were able to give or teach someone else; some moment when you failed, but moved on; a lesson you learned or a skill you mastered; an unexpected gift you received; a goal you achieved; or some other surprising circumstance. Write for about ten minutes. As quickly as possible, describe the moment or event in chronological order first, providing as much detail as you can.

Once you have two pages:

- Give your narrative to a reader who will ask questions in the margins (and maybe annotate the text). These questions may be journalistic: who, what, when, where, and why? Or they may be sensory: what smells, tastes, sounds, sights, or textures do you associate with this moment or event? Or they may ask for specific details, such as responses, reactions, or dialogue.

- Change to a different color of ink and begin adding answers to your reader's questions, trying to give rich, sensory detail.

- Consider changing the order of the telling. Experiment by beginning the short write in the middle of the story (or the end) and use flashbacks and foreshadowing to help the reader anticipate what happens next.

- Consider different genres you might use to tell your story. How would the different pieces connect?

VIVID DESCRIPTION

One key element of a good story is vivid description. In other words, writing in a way that helps your audience see what you see. Now that you have some form of a draft, you can begin to play with the description in it to help a reader "be with you" in the story.

Here's a simple activity to help demonstrate the concept.

First, think about the place where you spend the most time every day. Is it your dorm room? Maybe it's your apartment? The library?

Now, if you were in that space right now, what would you see?

_____

_____

_____

What sounds would you be likely to hear?

_____

_____

_____

What about smells? What sorts of smells would be in the air?

_____

_____

_____

What about taste? This one might not seem as relevant, but give it a try. Maybe you eat pizza in your dorm room a lot. Describe the taste.

_____

_____

_____

Finally, think about touch. What sorts of things could you touch in that place? Soft, warm bedsheets? The bright blue rug in the center of the floor? The delicately curved keys on your computer keyboard? Write about it.

_____

_____

_____

Great! Now think about doing this activity for each and every place that appears in your narrative—as an exercise, go back into your down draft and identify each place, practicing adding details. You may not use all of the writing you create from this activity, but the point is that you will have a lot of writing to draw from. You'll just need to make decisions about what information will be most memorable and meaningful for your readers to help them live with you in your story.

TENSION AND TURN

Tension and turn are important elements to any good story, too. Without them, readers are left with narratives that are more like lists than anything else. Did you ever write a "What I Did on My Summer Vacation" essay in which you simply told the audience the activities from your summer vacation—one by one? Boring! A good story slows down and speeds up, zooms in and out, or builds in detail and description, depending on the importance of the action.

To develop tension in a story, there are several basic things you can do.

First, identify a goal. If you think about the television shows, books, or movies that you enjoy most you'll probably realize that each one does a good job at creating tension. The main character—or protagonist—has some goal that he or she is trying to reach whether it's destroying an evil ring, saving the planet, or surviving a zombie apocalypse.

Second, create some doubt. For the tension to really rise, the audience has to be left wondering whether or not the protagonist is going to achieve her or his goal.

Third, describe the turning point. The turning point is that moment in a story where things reach a climax, allowing the story to move into a resolution and conclusion.

Now, in the space below, try to do this for your own narrative.

1. Identify the goal of the main character—most likely, you.

2. Identify the source of tension in your narrative. Try writing it as a question. For example, "Will Edgar finish his narrative before time runs out?"

3. Identify the turning point where things were "do or die" or "now or never" or when you came to some new realization.

Once you have identified these aspects, you can decide where to add more detail and importance in your draft. If this strategy doesn't seem to fully work with the draft you have, you can even try this out for other narrative ideas. Who knows? You might discover that one story proves to be even more interesting once you think about it.

_____

_____

_____

_____

_____

_____

_____

_____

_____

_____

Activity: Peer Review

Your draft in process is probably ready for a reader at this stage—and you're probably ready to read someone else's work besides your own.

First, identify anything in your draft that you think needs attention. You can make marginal notes, ask questions, or select specific aspects of the paper where you want a reader to focus. This will help you think more deeply about your needs as a writer, and it will help your reviewer focus feedback to help you.

Next, trade drafts with a partner, and spend some time as a reader giving feedback to help improve and deepen your partner's writing, taking cues from the directions and questions your partner provides.

Read through your partner's essay and along the way, *annotate*:

- Mark where you're confused, or where the writing is unclear (﹏﹏ wavy line beneath problematic sentences)

- Mark where writing is strong (✓ check mark next to outstanding sentences)

- Mark where you feel there should be expanded text or more detail (+ plus sign where there should be more)

On a blank sheet of paper, write:

- Name of Writer:

- Name of Reviewer:

Then answer the following questions:

- Did the opening paragraph catch your attention or was there part of it that could be cut? (There often is something that can be cut in rough drafts.)

- What story has the author chosen to tell?

- What were some of the sensory details, description, or imagery that you liked? Where could the writer include more details?

- Does the essay focus in on *a scene or specific moment* from the writer's experiences? Should the story be focused more on one incident/cut down in its scope?

- Why does the writer want to tell this story and why should the reader want to read it?

- Does the author use multiple genres to tell the story? Should s/he? Why or why not?

- How does the essay's organization (or lack of organization) help or hurt the writer's ability to communicate the central idea? How else might the writer organize the story?

- Does the writer use any clichés or sentimental moments? How can these be more unique?

- What suggestions do you have for a catchy title?

- What other suggestions can you provide?

Return the marked-up essay and the answers to these questions to the essay's author.

UNDERSTANDING AND USING FEEDBACK

Interpreting feedback and translating it into specific things to do for your writing can be a challenging aspect of improving as a writer.

- What do you do if your instructor doesn't give you a list of specific things to improve?

- What do you do if you disagree with feedback that your instructor gives you?

- What do you do if the person giving you feedback is a novice writer like you?

To help you navigate this challenging, and sometimes frustrating, part of the writing process, here are a few important principles to keep in mind.

1. **Own Your Writing**. Your writing is just that—yours. You are in charge of what it says and how it says it. That means you make decisions about which suggestions you act on and what suggestions you use or ignore. If your instructor suggests changes that you are uncertain about, you should talk to your instructor. Find out more about why he or she made that suggestion. Explain your own rationale to your instructor. In most cases, a disagreement can lead to a deeper understanding of writing, rhetoric, and conventions. Relatedly, remember that feedback you give to others does not obligate them to make changes—the writing belongs to the writer, to change, to share, and to publish.

2. **Collect Multiple Perspectives.** One of the most common concerns when it comes to feedback is knowing when someone is making a good, overall suggestion and when that person is just making a suggestion based on their own preferences or (mis)perceptions about what good writing looks like. To make sure that you're not being led down the wrong path, talk to multiple engaged readers and ask specific questions. If four out of five classmates think your introduction needs more action, then that might be a sign it needs some work. If only one person out of ten can't identify your main idea, then you can be pretty confident that your main idea is clear.

In the space below, describe the most helpful feedback you ever received on your writing. What did the person say? How did he or she say it? Use this memory of helpful feedback to tailor your questions for a reader and to shape the kind of feedback you give to others.

_____

_____

_____

_____

_____

_____

_____

_____

_____

_____

Reflective Cover Memo

Date: _____

To (Instructor's Name): _____

From (Author of Paper): _____

Subject: Reflection on "Final for Now" Version of [List Title of Paper Below]

_____

Reflective Cover Memo for "Final for Now"— Personal Narrative

Writing Process. Please reflect on your writing process. What did you try for the first time? What comments from peer workshop and conferences did you explore in your revision? How did this improve your paper? Please cite concrete examples.

_____

_____

_____

_____

_____

_____

Purpose and Audience. What were you trying to accomplish in this piece of writing? What audience do you envision? How do you know you achieved your purpose and reached your audience, or, if you're not sure, what kind of feedback do you need to get there?

_____

_____

_____

_____

_____

_____

Narrative Conventions and Trouble Spots. This chapter has identified specific writing techniques for this paper. How, for you, is narrative different from other kinds of writing? What are the conventions of narratives, and how do they show up in your writing? What were your trouble spots with this project? How did you deal with these trouble spots? What did you learn from composing this project?

_____

_____

_____

_____

_____

_____

Future Writing. What plans do you have for revisions of this paper for the Final Portfolio draft? For instance, what else might you have discussed if you had more time/space? What would you do differently?

_____

_____

_____

_____

_____

Questions or Comments. What questions do you have for your instructor about the construction of your paper or the writing process? What would you like your instructor to focus on while reading the "Final for Now" version of this paper?

_____

_____

_____

_____

_____

Reflective Cover Memo

Date: September 15, 2017

To: English 101 Instructors and Students

From: Sarah Morris

Subject: Reflection on "Final for Now" Version of Lost and Found at Coopers Rock

Reflective Cover Memo for "Final for Now"— Personal Narrative

Writing Process. Please reflect on your writing process. What did you try for the first time? What comments from peer workshop and conferences did you explore in your revision? How did this improve your paper? Please cite concrete examples.

This paper was very hard for me to write. I wanted to write about some big, dramatic story, and I just couldn't find one to write about, so I tried to weave together several small stories about a place that is important to me. Based on reader comments, I was able to develop some more details, especially trying to remember specifics, like my grandmother's face. I can't really remember what she looked like, so I looked at family albums and used my imagination—I made choices to embellish some details to make my memories seem sharper and clearer for a reader. Writing about memories is hard, so I had to try to piece together one story out of a lot of memories, which was a challenge for me because I wanted to tell the truth, but I couldn't remember an exact day—I had to focus on the truth of how things felt instead of the fact of the moment. An example of this is the paragraph just after the story about my grandmother getting lost.

Purpose and Audience. What were you trying to accomplish in this piece of writing? What audience do you envision? How do you know you achieved your purpose and reached your audience, or, if you're not sure, what kind of feedback do you need to get there?

I started out wanting to tell a funny family story that I remembered from my childhood and that is told in my family. I didn't really know at first why this story, but as I wrote I found that I wanted to portray an image of a place and stories that took place in that space in order to help a reader see its importance. I think I'm writing for an audience of readers like me who know the place—but also those who don't because maybe it can help educate them about how special West Virginia's parks are and how important it is to have a place that's wild to escape. I also wanted to remember that I'm writing for English 101 readers, too, so this piece of writing is a teaching tool as well as a personal narrative. I don't know if my audience will understand the power of place I want to convey, so I might need help making sure I have a clear thesis—but also one that isn't too preachy or oversimplified.

Narrative Conventions and Trouble Spots. This chapter has identified specific writing techniques for this paper. How, for you, is narrative different from other kinds of writing? What are the conventions of narratives, and how do they show up in your writing? What were your trouble spots with this project? How did you deal with these trouble spots? What did you learn from composing this project?

Narrative is very difficult for me to write (and I think that shows in this piece). I have a hard time telling stories about myself that have a "so what?" moment. I think I may have chosen a moment or story that is too small and irrelevant. It doesn't have the kind of "tension and turn" that a really dramatic story (like the kind in a death of a family member or winning a big game). I do think this piece tells a couple of different stories with a series of events, but I'm not sure the events come to a climax like the "witch hat"model says they should. I tried to show that small stories are important in the way we learn about ourselves, too, but I'm not sure I was successful. I learned that writing about myself is hard. My biggest trouble spot here was finding something interesting about my life to write about that could also appeal to my audience.

Future Writing. What plans do you have for revisions of this paper for the Final Portfolio draft? For instance, what else might you have discussed if you had more time/space? What would you do differently?

If I had more time, I might go back to my family members to see if the memory I have is as accurate as their memories of this event. I know it must be important because I remember it so vividly, but I am not sure why. I feel like I discussed too much, and that maybe I should narrow to just one story, but I am not sure how to do that.

Questions or Comments. What questions do you have for your instructor about the construction of your paper or the writing process? What would you like your instructor to focus on while reading the "Final for Now" version of this paper?

I guess I want to know if my paper meets the assignment guidelines first. Also, I want to know whether the story comes across as I want it to. Does it show how the place is almost a setting or character in the story of my life, and is this concept too cliche? I want good feedback that will help me connect to readers. Is the story cohesive enough or are the multiple stories here confusing? Is the "so what?" clear? Is the ending OK, or is it too neatly tied into a "lesson"? How do I make this piece more relevant and connected to the assignment?

Using this Piece in English 101. What do you want English 101 students and teachers to know about this piece of writing? How do you want them to use this text in classrooms?

I want teachers and students to see my example narrative as an imperfect draft and as a work in progress. It's not a polished piece yet, and it's definitely not "the right way" or the only way to do a personal narrative. In classes, I want students and teachers to be able to have a useful conversation about what the piece of writing does well—and also about what it can do better. I want it to be a starting point for learning and discussion (and not an endpoint for what the writing could or should look like).

SAMPLE NARRATIVE

Sarah Morris   Morris   1

Professor Sura

ENGL 101

September 15, 2017

Lost and Found at Coopers Rock

My earliest memory of a public forest was when Great-Grandma Morris, my dad's grandmother, got lost at Coopers Rock State Park. I was about four years old. The whole family was visiting, including my father's cousins, aunts, uncles, parents, and grandparents. Our small house was full of people I had never met before, doors and windows open to combat the heat of the summer days in West Virginia. That afternoon, a group of us headed to the nearby state park, one of our county's most spectacular attractions, to take a walk, look down on the Cheat River, and get a reprieve from the heat. It was always about ten degrees cooler on Cheat Mountain.

When we got there, we all stood on the overlook, and the adults talked about CCC construction, pointed at spots on the horizon, smokestacks in the distance, a boat on the river. Someone held my hand to keep me from going too close to the rough-hewn plank fencing that lined the edge of the rock face to protect visitors from stepping over the rim and tumbling hundreds of feet down. Someone else gave me a coin, so I could look through the distance viewer out across the hillside; I was too small to reach it, so another someone held me up.

We milled around for a while, taking in the scenery, until someone asked, "Where's Grandma?" She was nowhere on the overlook, nor out on the pathways leading up to it. The adults fanned out into a search, calling her name(s): "Momma!" "Grandma!" "GRANDMA!" The urgency rose as people walked farther away from the overlook, combing the woods and trails.

Morris   2

I remember standing on the wooden footbridge spanning across a ravine that separated two large rocks, one on the main path and one that leads out to the overlook where we had been. I heard Great-Grandma calling back to us. "Here I am!" she called, oblivious to the urgency of the situation—everyone thought she was lost. I pressed my forehead against the railing, looking down, and there she was, in the ravine below me. She was smiling at me, looking up, creases deepening around her eyes, between the rocks and rhododendrons, on a path we didn't see. She repeated herself, "Here I am!" and this time, she waved, still smiling.

I tugged the shirttail of the nearest adult, pointed, and a chorus of relieved talk replaced the worried chatter. "There you are!" Aunt Madeline yelled, "How did you get down there?"

Grandma looked around, her white curls bouncing. "I don't know," she said. After some exploration of pathways, a cousin found the way down to her and brought her back along the path to the overlook. She wasn't lost, she said, she could see and hear us the whole time—she knew exactly where she was.

This was my first memory of Coopers Rock, a park that seemed, as I grew older, to be an extension of my own backyard, as it probably does for many people who grow up in Monongalia and Preston Counties. My family went on walks and took picnics, fished in the trout pond, swung on the swings. I found painted box turtles in the woods, scared ruffed grouse from the underbrush, heard pileated woodpeckers laughing in the treetops, discovered mysterious plants like Indian Pipe, and startled countless deer, who would bound away, leaping through the thickets. I saw my first rattlesnake at Coopers Rock, and I learned to trail run at Coopers Rock. It was a place of discovery and wonder, and, even though I grew up far from town, it was different from our yard and surrounding woods. There were trails, for one,

NOTES

streams and ponds, and huge rocks, covered with moss and lichen, and dramatic views at every turn. I would be moving along a path, closed in on both sides by trees and mountain laurel, and the next moment the leaves would part, the path emerging on the lip of a cliff, looking far out over the Cheat. I have always loved Coopers Rock.

After I moved away from Morgantown, and before I came back home, I regularly left early on trips back home to run on the roadside trail. After crossing over the state line on I-68, Coopers Rock was the first stop I made, and taking the exit ramp off the highway was my first taste of home. Pulling the car into the first parking lot, I laced up my trail shoes, ate a snack, grabbed a water bottle, and headed down the Scott's Run Trail. After a couple of hours in the car, legs stiff, it felt good to kick through the muck, loosening up. The mud stuck to my shoes and spattered my legs; the first downgrade of the trail is always wet and torn up by tires of mountain bikes. At the bottom of the hill, the trail leveled out, opening up into and rolling along the streambed, rocky and interwebbed with roots. I kept close track of my footing, looking up at boulders and mountain laurels lining the stream and trail, listening to the rushing water, and sinking into the woods and into myself. The uphill climb out of the stream bed got my heart pumping, and I had to be careful not to slip on the loose rocks. Sometimes I saw coyote tracks, and once, the unmistakable print of a bear.

Often, this run, between the city where I attended college and my home that I missed, opened my breath and turned me inward: it felt like a doorway into my real self, the place I belonged. I finished these runs sweaty and giddy, caked with clay and salt and a feeling of wholeness. I toweled off, drove the last 20 miles barefoot, opened the door to my parents' house looking like I had been dragged through the dirt.

I have always loved Coopers Rock, and my life is filled with stories like these: small moments that connect me to the place and also define my understanding of the world and the people in it. Coopers Rock continues to shape my life. When my childhood friend's son died, we hiked the Raven Rock trail to the overlook there. Vultures circled above us, the river rushed by below, and under the buzz of the powerlines we drank whisky from a flask, ate chocolate, and cried.

When my niece comes to visit, we always take a day to explore, picking a trail, carrying binoculars and bird and plant identification guides, and packing a bagged lunch. She records our findings in her nature journal, inventing spellings and pressing leaves into the pages.

I hike with my partner and our dog, who we let off leash once we're far enough to not disturb other hikers. A long-legged, mixed-breed rescue mutt, she runs circles away and back, crashing through the underbrush, bringing back sticks to throw, and panting, wild-eyed.

There isn't one single story that defines my relationship with Coopers Rock as a place, and yet, it's a setting intertwined into the story of my life. This is true, I assume, for others, too: weddings at the overlook, children on the playground, reunions in the pavillions (built by grandfathers in the CCC), afternoons fishing, hunting trips, interpretive hikes, first kisses, family, friendships… Coopers Rock is more than a state park. It's a green jewel on the map, and maybe even a sacred space. Regardless, I know this: like Great-Grandma Morris, when I'm there, I can see and hear, I know exactly where I am, and I know I'm not lost.

Telling Someone Else's Story

In this chapter, you will move from writing about yourself to writing about someone (or something) else.

GETTING STARTED

People often read stories to learn about other people, places, events, or organizations. Making a story about other things and people is an act of meaning making. This chapter asks you to tell a story about another person, place, or thing that matters to you or that you would like to learn about. Write a story that can inform others, too.

PURPOSE

The purpose of this assignment is to build on what you've learned about description and organization while changing perspective. Instead of telling your own story, you now have to tell someone (or something) else's story. Here are a few additional goals for this chapter:

- Recognize and analyze the ethical issues involved in representing others.

- Conduct primary research in the form of an interview.

- Conduct secondary research in order to understand your subject's context.

- Integrate other voices into your writing—through summary, paraphrase, and quotation.

AUDIENCE

Your instructor may have specific instructions about what audience to write for. Otherwise, consider what sort of newspaper, magazine, or website would likely publish a story on your topic. Do some critical thinking, research, and reading of examples to help you imagine that audience.

CONVENTIONS

One common genre for this type of writing is the profile. Typically, profiles provide an in-depth description of a person, place, organization, or event. They help a reader see the profile's subject in a more complex way, often uncovering elements of the subject that are unexpected or unique. For example, a profile of a famous movie star might describe how the person is "down to earth" or supports several humanitarian causes. A profile contains elements of narrative, too. Profiles can incorporate vivid description as well as tension.

Like narratives, there are many ways a profile might be organized. Listen for your instructor to give you specific instructions about how to organize your story.

TROUBLE SPOTS

One thing to avoid is turning in an interview transcript. Your profile should sound more like your narrative and less like a back and forth discussion where you write the question and then write the person's answer. A transcript can be a useful tool for your profile, but you shouldn't turn it in as your actual profile.

ASSESSMENT

Your instructor may adjust the criteria below to fit the specific project for your course. In any case, here are a few key criteria to keep in mind:

- This paper will propose a strong and appropriate topic.

- This paper will find an appropriate interview subject.

- This paper will use description to fully contextualize your subject.

- This paper will introduce quoted material smoothly and correctly.

- This paper will use an engaging and audience-appropriate tone of voice.

- This paper will document any sources (including your interview) ethically and accurately through in-text citations and a Works Cited list (using guidelines found in *Easy Writer*).

- This paper will be approximately 1,200 to 1,500 words (4–5 pages) of polished writing.

MIND MAPPING

Do you remember when Chapter 1 mentioned that invention was the name given to activities that help writers come up with ideas? Freewriting was the example in the last chapter. This chapter introduces you to mind mapping, which you're probably already familiar with. This activity is also frequently called clustering, or simply, brainstorming.

It's a straightforward activity. You simply write a word in the middle of a sheet of paper and then add words and ideas that relate to it. The example below focuses on the start of a mind map that might help you choose a focus for your profile. There are a few blank boxes so that you can write in your own ideas.

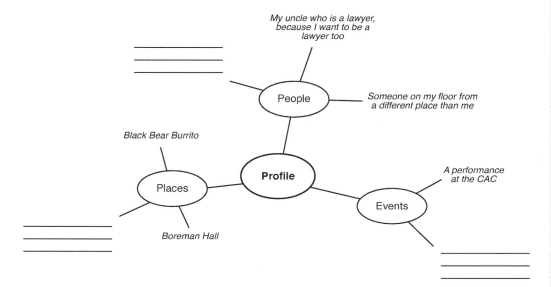

Great! Now why don't you take a few minutes to create a mind map of your own? You can choose anything. If you're having trouble coming up with something, try making a mind map of interesting places at WVU.

FINDING YOUR ANGLE

The most important element of the profile is your angle. You may also think of this as your thesis, issue, or central focus. Think of angle this way: Your topic is the subject—person, place, event, organization—that you're writing about, but your angle is the specific focus that makes your topic the most interesting to an audience. Often the best angles challenge preconceptions that audiences have for a subject.

For example, one WVU student chose to write about the school's rifle team (topic). The student then focused the story on the perspective of the only female member of the team (angle).

Journalists get articles published by presenting a commonly covered issue or event in a new way. All the assignments in this course encourage critical thinking. You may want to start with a question or understanding of how people see the work, event, issue, etc. you are discussing and think of a way you can talk about it differently.

You will want to make sure you come up with a topic and angle *before* your interview. That way, you can brainstorm a list of open-ended questions to bring with you. Sometimes after you conduct an interview, you might see your angle shift a bit, and that is OK. During your interview, you might gain new insights that lead you to a clearer idea of what might work for your angle based on the answers you receive and conversations you have.

ASKING FOR AN INTERVIEW

The interview is a critical piece of the profile project. In order to give yourself enough time to complete the interview and write your final-for-now paper, you should ask your subject if and when he/she is available several weeks before the project is due. Here is an e-mail template you might use to politely request an interview with your subject:

Dear <PERSON'S TITLE (if applicable) AND FULL NAME>,

I am student at West Virginia University taking English 101. One of my formal writing assignments for the semester requires that I select a topic and conduct an interview with someone involved with that topic. I have chosen to focus on <TOPIC> because _____. I am writing to you because _____, and I am hoping that you will please consider meeting with me for a formal sit-down (or phone/skype) interview sometime before <DATE>. The interview should take no longer than thirty minutes, and it can be scheduled at a time convenient for you. Thank you for your time and consideration.

Sincerely,

<YOUR NAME>

Activity: Writing Interview Questions

Interviews are a form of what is called **field research**. Typically, the person or people you interview have specific knowledge or perspectives on a subject that are valuable to your work. In *Easy Writer*, Andrea Lunsford suggests that before interviewing someone, a researcher should have a list of "factual and open-ended questions" to ask.

Consider your topic. What sorts of fact-based questions would be appropriate to ask as part of your interview? Write a few of them here.

_____

_____

_____

_____

_____

_____

Now, consider what sorts of open-ended questions would be appropriate to ask as part of your interview? Write a few of them here.

_____

_____

_____

_____

_____

_____

_____

For more on interviews and field research see section 13e of *Easy Writer*.

HOW TO USE INTERVIEW TRANSCRIPTS

After you complete an interview it will be helpful to transcribe the questions and the answers into a document so that you can use the interview as source material for your profile. You might use the interview material in several ways.

1. **Direct Quoting:** Turn your transcript over so you can't see it. Attempt to recall, from memory, any direct quotes that were particularly striking. If possible, list them on the back of your transcript or a separate sheet of paper. Afterward, check your transcript and see what else you may want to directly quote and mark the passages.

2. **Paraphrase and Summary:** Next, using your transcript, go through and decide what you may want to paraphrase or summarize. Remember that paraphrasing typically involves taking all the main points and rewording the ideas yourself. Look for the places in your interview that would be best served by this method. On your transcript, mark each passage in a way that makes sense to you. You might find that some of the questions you asked and answers you received aren't as relevant to the angle as you initially thought they were. Remember it is almost certain that you won't use every aspect of your interview and that's OK.

Activity: Writing a Lead

The first paragraph has to do a lot of work: it must grab the readers' interest, provide enough context to tell them what they will be reading about, and encourage them to continue reading.

Writers often call this beginning a "lead." The goal in writing a strong lead is to convince a casual reader to stop scanning and actually read the whole article. This is the reason it needs to be interesting. A strong lead should do the following:

- Capture the readers' imaginations by raising questions.

- Contain some essence of the story. Readers should have some sense of what the story is about and why they should care.

- Set the mood and tone—is this going to be a funny story, tragic, hard-hitting, or celebratory?

- Be as concise as possible. In other words, it should cover all these points quickly and powerfully. Think short and punchy. Most leads are, at most, 25 to 30 words. (This last point was 30 words.)

The good news is that the lead doesn't have to be the first thing you write (and it does sometimes run longer than 30 words). Try a few different leads—and be sure to get some feedback—before you settle on the right one.

TYPES OF LEADS

Try writing one version of each type of lead as you think about the introduction for your own profile.

Summary Lead: Summarizes the most important/newsworthy elements in the story (typically in one sentence)—the Who, What, Where, When, and Why. It is also known as the standard lead, and is the most common.

_____

_____

_____

_____

_____

_____

Single-Item Lead: Concentrates on just one or two of the 5 Ws for a bigger punch.

_____

_____

_____

_____

_____

_____

Cartridge Lead: Uses one word or a short phrase as a teaser for the rest of the lead. Often, this can seem gimmicky, and this tactic should be used artfully and sparingly, if at all.

_____

_____

_____

_____

_____

_____

Question Lead: Poses a question to the reader, which the story proceeds to answer. This can also seem gimmicky and should be used sparingly. If used, it needs to be followed up by the necessary contextual information.

_____

_____

_____

_____

_____

_____

Anecdotal Lead: Makes use of story and description to draw the reader in.

_____

_____

_____

_____

_____

Activity: Reading Like a Writer—Profile

For this activity you will read a sample profile and answer a few questions about it. Use the sample student profile at the end of this chapter to help you, or your instructor may ask you to read a different example.

Title of Article: _____

Author: _____

Source: _____

Purpose. What is the author trying to accomplish with this article? How do you know? List details from the article that help you to understand the purpose.

_____

_____

_____

_____

_____

_____

Audience. Who do you think this profile is written for? Be as specific as you can in terms of age, gender, occupation, and characteristics like that.

_____

_____

_____

_____

_____

_____

Conventions. What sorts of conventions do you notice in terms of things like formatting or content?

_____

_____

_____

_____

_____

_____

_____

What about the lead? Explain how the article tries to "hook" your interest.

_____

_____

_____

_____

_____

_____

What about how the profile ends? Explain how the author brings the article to a conclusion.

_____

_____

_____

_____

_____

_____

Workshop:
Peer Review for the Profile

Author:_____

Title: _____

Reader: _____

In this workshop, **you will be a magazine editor.** You will work in groups to do the kind of round-table editing/ responding that real publishers and editors do all the time. Your group will be given papers belonging to other students in the class (you will not read your group members' papers) and you will read them and respond to them imagining that you are the editors addressed in the cover letters, committed to publishing these profiles in your magazine. What does the writer still need to do to grab and keep the audience's attention? How is the author's research? How well has the author cited sources? Is the author's interview in-depth and engaging? Does the author use exciting, vivid description to bring the person, place, or event to life for the reader?

Step One: You should be in groups of two to four for this workshop, though no group will be given more than three papers to read. Begin by physically moving so you can easily talk to all your group members. Introduce yourselves. Now each of you pick up a paper and begin reading. Read the whole paper without marking on it. Then make a few notes in the space provided for "Reader 1." When you are done, pass the paper and the comment sheet to a group member and proceed to the next paper, reading and making notes until everyone in the group has read all the papers.

Step Two: Discuss the papers, assigning one person to take notes in the space provided for "Group Feedback." Go through the papers in any order you like, responding to the concerns suggested. Also feel free to add any suggestions or points of praise that your group feels are warranted. And if the group members disagree, note that too (e.g., *some of us thought your interview was a bit short and lacked depth, but other members of the group thought it was sufficient*).

Here are the things to make notes on for each paper:

- How well does the introduction grab your attention? How could it be improved?

- Does the writer use vivid, exciting language throughout? Is something particularly well evoked or missing (e.g., a description of a person or place)?

- How well does the interview (or interviews) work here? Is it Q&A format, are quotes poorly incorporated or not memorable, is there enough interview material?

- Is the writer's research integrated well? Cited? Could it be done more smoothly? Is there background information missing that you wish was included?

- Does this article KEEP your attention all the way to the end? How? How could it be made more engaging?

Paper Title: _____ **Author:** _____

Reader 1

Reader 2

Reader 3

Group Feedback

Reflective Cover Memo

Date: _____

To (Instructor's Name): _____

From (Author of Paper): _____

Subject: Reflection on "Final for Now" Version of [List Title of Paper Below]

_____

Reflective Cover Memo for "Final for Now"—Profile

Writing Process. Please reflect on your writing process. What did you try for the first time? What comments from peer workshop and conferences did you explore in your revision? How did this improve your paper? Please cite concrete examples.

_____

_____

_____

_____

_____

_____

Feature. How did your own identity and experience influence the way you viewed your subject? What questions do you wish you had asked— what could have been done differently? What did you find most challenging about this project—and how did you deal with those challenges?

_____

_____

_____

_____

_____

_____

Organizing into an Article. How did you decide the focus of your article? What was your focus? What quotes and observations did you use to focus your article? How did you do this? Talk about how you handled quotes and details effectively and where this may have been difficult. Did you use any images? Why or why not?

_____

_____

_____

_____

_____

_____

Future Writing. What plans do you have for revisions of this paper for the final portfolio draft? What else might you have discussed in the profile if you had more time/space?

_____

_____

_____

_____

_____

_____

_____

Questions or Comments. What questions do you have for your instructor about the construction of your paper or the writing process? What would you like your instructor to focus on while reading the "Final for Now" version of this paper?

_____

_____

_____

_____

_____

_____

Reflective Cover Memo

Date: October 5, 2017

To: English 101 Instructors and Students

From: Emma DiPasquale

Subject: Reflection on "Final for Now" Version of For the Love of Forests

Reflective Cover Memo for "Final for Now"—Profile

Writing Process. Please reflect on your writing process. What did you try for the first time? What comments from peer workshop and conferences did you explore in your revision? How did this improve your paper? Please cite concrete examples.

This paper was hard for me to write. I had never learned about angles, and I wasn't sure if I selected a good one based on my topic. I had also never integrated direct quotes into a paper before. It was hard to decide which quotes would be interesting to readers, but after going through peer review, I cut some out and was satisfied with the few I left in. My peer review partner told me I could probably develop a more catchy lead, but I decided to keep the one I had because I couldn't think of anything else yet. I would like to work on that for the portfolio. My partner also told me to explain certain terms and topics in more detail, such as the WVLT and BoPARC. I didn't have a complete draft for my conference or peer review session, which made it difficult to get a lot of feedback. My goal going forward is to have complete drafts for both of those meetings.

Feature. How did your own identity and experience influence the way you viewed your subject? What questions do you wish you had asked— what could have been done differently? What did you find most challenging about this project—and how did you deal with those challenges?

I'm not from West Virginia and am not very outdoorsy, but after meeting Dr. Landenberger on a field trip for another class I really wanted to learn more. I think that really influenced me to stick with this topic. I know land is very important in West Virginia and exploring it seems to be a big part of WVU's culture.

I think the interview portion was definitely the most challenging part of this project. I'm kind of a shy person, and I have never interviewed anyone else before, so it was hard for me to interrupt or ask Dr. Landenberger to speak more after it seemed like he was done answering. I don't necessarily wish I had asked more or different questions, but rather asked Dr. Landenberger to explain the things he did mention in more detail.

Organizing into an Article. How did you decide the focus of your article? What was your focus? What quotes and observations did you use to focus your article? How did you do this? Talk about how you handled quotes and details effectively and where this may have been difficult. Did you use any images? Why or why not?

I wanted to write about Dr. Landenberger because he is really cool and passionate about his work. I wanted to focus on his current job, but he had done so many things I felt I lost my angle. I tried to use quotes that directly related to his current work, how he received his current job, or things that represented his passion for his job. I didn't use any images, but I might experiment with that for the portfolio because it could be really cool to see images of the projects he is working on and the different landscapes.

Future Writing. What plans do you have for revisions of this paper for the final portfolio draft? What else might you have discussed in the profile if you had more time/space?

I am planning on conducting a follow-up interview with Dr. Landenberger if he is available. I think it would be helpful to get more information on the projects he is working on in his current role so I can shift my angle a bit. I don't think there is anything else I would've discussed since I found it difficult to reach the minimum word count with the information I had.

Questions or Comments. What questions do you have for your instructor about the construction of your paper or the writing process? What would you like your instructor to focus on while reading the "Final for Now" version of this paper?

I guess I want to know whether or not this paper really reads like a profile. As I was proofreading it, I couldn't tell if this was a piece that might be featured in a magazine or another professional publication. I also want to know how I can better focus this paper and what other specific details need to be included as they relate to Dr. Landenberger's work/projects.

Using this Piece in English 101. What do you want English 101 students and teachers to know about this piece of writing? How do you want them to use this text in classrooms?

I want teachers and students to see my example profile as an unfocused draft. This draft is in its early stages despite being a "final-for-now" piece. I hope this draft generates a constructive conversation about the strengths and weaknesses of the draft, and what I could change before submitting the piece in the portfolio. I want this to be an example of what an early draft might look like, not necessarily what the finished product will be.

SAMPLE PROFILE

Emma DiPasquale

DiPasquale   1

Professor Sura

ENGL 101

5 October 2017

For the Love of Forests

Trees. That is Dr. Rick Landenberger's specialty. Landenberger is a forest ecologist who has experience in natural resource management and protected area management. Though Landenberger has always been interested and active in the outdoors, he initially started out at as a business major at the State University of New York College at Plattsburgh.

"I was initially interested in working in the ski industry as a sales rep, selling equipment. But, after one semester of business and marketing courses, I changed my major to ecology and never looked back," says Landenberger. "I was always interested in the natural world but didn't have much of an idea about working in the environmental field until I took an introduction to environmental science course. That changed my life."

Landenberger continued his education at State University of New York College of Environmental Sciences and Forestry, earning his master of science in forest resource management. After working for a few years for the US Forest Service on the Monongahela National Forest as a wilderness ranger on the Cheat, Potomac, and Greenbrier Ranger Districts, he went back to school in 1994 to earn his Ph.D. in forest science at West Virginia University. In 1999, Landenberger took a post-doctoral research position in Ecology and Remote Sensing, splitting his time between the Departments of Biology and Geology & Geography. His work has addressed detection and ecology of invasive plants, such as Ailanthus (tree of heaven), censusing a threatened species, and mapping of native trees in the mixed-mesophytic forest.

Now, Landenberger splits his time between WVU's Department of Geology & Geography and the West Virginia Land Trust, where he works as the science and land management specialist. Founded in 1995, the West Virginia Land Trust (WVLT) is a statewide nonprofit organization dedicated to protecting West Virginia's natural lands, scenic areas, water quality, and recreational access. Their mission, as stated on their website, is to protect land with significant conservation values through the use of conservation easements and real estate acquisitions, and by working with a state-wide network of partners to build a passionate land conservation movement in the state. Since 1995, the WVLT has protected or facilitated the protection of more than 7,000 acres of land in the state of West Virginia ("Our Work").

Additionally, the WVLT works to protect land through a variety of ways, including: placing permanent conservation easements on properties (or the right to use and/or enter onto the real property of another without possessing it); purchasing land through real estate acquisitions; accepting land donations; administering grants and loans to partner organizations; providing technical assistance to landowners interested in managing their property more sustainably; educating and informing the public about land protection tools; supporting the development of laws and regula-tions that promote and benefit land and water conservation, and convening and facil-itating partnerships that build the capacity of communities throughout West Virginia to protect our state's land and water resources ("Our Work").

In his position, Landenberger writes management plans, monitors conser-vation easements and title restrictions, and works with volunteers and consultants on various land management and restoration projects such as trail building, invasive species removal, law enforcement, and more.

"I oversee the stewardship responsibilities of the WVLT," says Landenberger. "We own seven conservation properties (properties that are managed for soil, forest, and water conservation and restoration), and hold conservation easements on 20 more. I work on the land that we own, improving it and making accessible to the public for recreation, and with private landowners on their easements, helping to protect the soil and water on their farms and forests."

Over the four years Landenberger has held this position, he has helped contribute additions to the park system, raising awareness of green space values, and has assisted in building trails in the BoPARC system, or the Morgantown Board of Parks and Recreation. BoPARC is committed to providing a quality system of parks, trails, facilities, and programs that enhance the community and the well-being of residents. Landenberger has worked mostly at Marilla Park, which is home to the Marilla Recreation Center and Marilla Skate Park. The park is a 45-acre multipurpose area that also includes an outdoor pool with two water slides, youth baseball fields, tennis courts and basketball courts ("About"). The park also hosts a variety of summer camps, who Landenberger has worked with to help enhance the park. Just this past summer, with the help of the BoPARC summer camp kids, Landenberger was able to build a trail, connecting a neighborhood with the Deckers Creek Rail-Trail via a patch of older forest.

There are plenty of volunteer opportunities to get involved with some of WVLT's projects. Landenberger completes trail work on both Morgantown's Elizabeth's Woods Nature Preserve and Charleston's Wallace Hartman Nature Preserve. The Elizabeth's Woods Nature Preserve is an 84-acre wooded sanctuary located just south of Morgantown. Volunteer projects include improving parking and accessibility, extending trail networks, adding interpretive signs, planning educational pro-

DiPasquale   4

grams, and conducting local history research. The Wallace Hartman Nature Preserve is a 52-acre natural area located minutes from downtown Charleston. Volunteer projects include improving parking and accessibility, clearing invasive species, maintaining and fortifying existing trails, extending trail networks, adding interpretive signs, and conducting local history research.

Landenberger recognizes the work he is doing as critical, and hopes others view it in a similar fashion."What is so important for people to remember about parks is that they provide many human ecosystem services like clean air and water, without which we'd all be even sicker, poorer, and dumber than we are now! Setting aside a few wild places pays huge dividends, many but not all of which are not included in contemporary economic thinking," says Landenberger.

Landenberger hopes the people of Monongalia County and West Virginia residents continue to take advantage of these green spaces and help preserve them in the ways they can."People have choices in where they live, and they are increasingly choosing places that have access to lots of public, protected land. That is a fact and speaks volumes to the value of parks and other green spaces."

Works Cited

"About Us—WV Land Trust." *West Virginia Land Trust*, http://www.wvlandtrust. org/about-us. Accessed 19 Jan. 2018.

Landenberger, Rick. Personal Interview. 18 Jan. 2018.

"Marilla Park." *BoPARC*. http://www.boparc.org/marilla-park.html. Accessed 19 Jan. 2018.

"Our Work—WV Land Trust." *West Virginia Land Trust*, http://www.wvlandtrust. org/projects/our-work/. Accessed 19 Jan. 2018.

CHAPTER 4
Writing to Reflect

This chapter asks you to take stock of what you've covered so far and practice for the final portfolio.

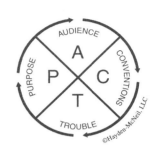

GETTING STARTED

PURPOSE

The primary purpose of this assignment is to reflect on how you've improved as a writer over the first half of the term. In fact, it's often helpful to imagine your portfolio as making an argument to your audience about how you've improved as a writer. In other words, the thesis of your midterm portfolio might be something like this:

"I have improved a little / somewhat / a lot over the first half of the term."

Your reflection, your projects, and your other writing are the evidence to support the claim you're making about your writing.

In addition to this primary purpose, there are a few other purposes that the midterm portfolio serves.

- It gives your instructor a chance to give you an in-progress grade for the course so that you know where your performance stands.

- It gives you practice putting a portfolio together before the final portfolio so that you can identify successful strategies and trouble spots before it really counts.

AUDIENCE

For this project, it often makes sense to focus on your instructor as your audience. After all, this is the point where your instructor moves from giving you feedback to improve your overall body of work to evaluating it according to the criteria in the book.

CONVENTIONS

Typical portfolios at the midterm contain a reflective element (for example, a memo, cover letter, or preface) along with copies of the first two projects in the course. Here are a few other characteristics of conventional portfolios:

- Reflective element is two to three pages long (600–900 words)

- Overall the portfolio is ten or more pages long (about 3,000–4,000 words)

TROUBLE SPOTS

Here are a few trouble spots regarding midterm portfolios. Think about what decisions you will make in order to address these questions:

- What can you use as evidence to support your purpose?

- How will you arrange your portfolio? What will come first, second, third, and so on?

- How can you make sure that your instructor doesn't miss important changes or developments to your writing? In other words, how can you shape the way your audience interacts with your work?

- How can you demonstrate your learning about the writing process?

ASSESSMENT

All English 101 courses have the same core criteria for evaluating portfolios. There are two places in this book that you can look at for portfolio evaluation criteria. The first is on the back inside cover of this book. This is really more of a checklist to help you think about and reflect on the course goals. The second place is the rubric on pages x–xiii that describes the criteria your instructor will use to evaluate your body of work.

For more on reflection read Sandra Giles's "Reflective Writing and the Revision Process: What Where You Thinking?"

MIDTERM REFLECTION

Date: _____

To: English 101 Class Members

From: English 101 Professor

Subject: Writer's Reflection at Midterm

Your ongoing project in English 101 is to develop your abilities as an effective reader, researcher, and writer. English 101 asks you to take stock of your progress in the class at the midterm point and again at the end of the semester as you submit your portfolio. Your reflection should take the form of a memo (about 3 pages long). This memo gives you a chance to do three things:

1. Consider your work as a writer, reader, and thinker.

2. Identify some personal writing goals for the remainder of the course (or beyond English 101).

3. Engage in a dialogue with the instructor about your writing.

Please use *specific examples* from your writing this semester to explain and illustrate the ways you've grown as a writer, reader, researcher, and thinker. To develop your points, think about what you've accomplished in your writing exercises, your projects, your responses to group members, and your responses to readings.

For additional ideas, try reviewing the readings for the class, the syllabus and assignment sheets, and the comments you've received from the instructor and your peers.

Drafting the Memo

The midterm memo should be about 3 pages long. As you draft, think about how you will organize information for the instructor:

*   What are the most important points/purposes that you want to convey?

*   What specific details will make your points both convincing and interesting?

*   How might *headings* help you group information and highlight key points?

*   How can you use the memo format, paragraph breaks, bullet points, verbal cues, and white space to help guide your instructor's reading?

*   Do you have control of your grammar, spelling, and punctuation? How about tone and style?

Keep in mind that the memo itself is another example of your writing. You may have a chance to work on it in class and to get feedback from your peers.

This assignment sheet (set up as a memo) offers you one example of some format and layout conventions; note the use of headings and bullet points, the spacing, etc. How does the memo format convey/shape the message and address audience in specific ways? How does a memo differ from an essay?

NOTES

Activity: Midterm Assessment of English 101

Instructor Name: _____ **Semester/Year:** _____

This course should be helping you develop and sharpen your writing abilities. Please take a moment at this midterm point to give your instructor some comments and ideas for meeting this goal.

Please respond to the following questions. You may remain anonymous if you like.

1. Which assignments and activities have been most helpful, informative, or useful for you? Please explain why.

   _____

   _____

   _____

   _____

   _____

   _____

   _____

   _____

2. Would you change any assignment or activity? Please explain why and suggest an improvement or alternative.

   _____

   _____

   _____

   _____

   _____

   _____

   _____

   _____

3. Are there any aspects of writing that you would like to learn more about?

   _____

   _____

   _____

   _____

   _____

   _____

   _____

4. How helpful are class periods, handouts, comments on rough drafts, conferences, and e-mail? Please explain.

_____

_____

_____

_____

_____

5. Do you have any additional comments or suggestions for improvement.

_____

_____

_____

_____

_____

Please use the space below or additional paper if you need more space.
Thank you for your input.

Analyzing the Story of a Text

Chapter 5 builds on what you've learned so far by taking a close look at analysis. That is, dividing something into its parts and explaining how those parts work together.

GETTING STARTED

PURPOSE

The purpose of this assignment is to practice what you've learned so far about rhetoric and apply it through analysis. Now you are writing a different kind of story. These stories will ask you to use what you've learned about description, context, and rhetoric to analyze something—in other words, to describe its parts and how those parts all work together. Another way to put it is to say that now you're going to tell a story about what something means.

AUDIENCE

Your instructor may have specific instructions about what audience to write for. Otherwise, consider writing for an audience like a family member or a friend. How would you explain rhetoric to that person? How would you explain the story of a text?

CONVENTIONS

Listen for your instructor to give you specific instructions about how to organize your text analysis. In general, you can expect to use an MLA format (see the sample paper in section 41e of *Easy Writer*). You can also expect to include elements like an introduction, a conclusion, a thesis statement, and a Works Cited page. Finally, you can expect that the body of your paper will do things like explain the context for what you are analyzing, describe what you are analyzing, and discuss how it attempts to persuade the audience through rhetorical strategies.

Hint: Don't spend a lot of time (or any time) telling your audience whether your text is great or awful; spend your time explaining how it tries to use things like emotions or logic to persuade an audience.

TROUBLE SPOTS

The text analysis might be a new genre to you, so at first it might be tough to figure out some of the basic elements. For example, what is a text? How do you identify logos, pathos, and ethos? What is the difference between arguing that something is good versus effective? Your previous work with rhetoric and your instructor will guide you through this project.

ASSESSMENT

Your instructor may adjust the criteria below to fit the specific project for your course. In any case, here are a few key criteria to keep in mind:

- This paper will include a thesis focused on the *rhetoric* of the text rather than the topic (how and why the text works—or fails to work—rather than a statement that simply says what the text is about).

- This paper will incorporate information that helps to contextualize what you're analyzing or supports your ideas about how the text works.

- This paper will be organized in a way that helps your reader understand what you analyzed and how it works.

- This paper will use well-developed examples, details, and facts based on close analysis.

- This paper will follow appropriate MLA guidelines.

- This paper will include approximately 1,200 to 1,500 words (4–5 pages) of polished writing.

Activity: Exploring and Analyzing Texts

Identifying Texts. Although "text" might make you think of something with writing, any object that can be analyzed is a text. Your instructor will guide you about what text to analyze for your paper, but it is useful to know some examples of common texts. Remember, this list is not exhaustive; use it to generate your own ideas about texts.

- Books
- Photographs
- Advertisements (both print ads and commercials)
- Movies
- Music videos
- TV clips
- Social media accounts

Analyzing Audience. Read words and images closely for a rhetorical analysis that focuses on audience issues.

- Search recent magazine covers online and compare two that seem wildly different. As you look at each cover, try to figure out who is the target audience for each. How can you tell? What specific examples or details can you point to as evidence? How could you create a thesis statement based on your observations and evidence?

Analyzing Purpose. Read words and images closely for a rhetorical analysis that focuses on purpose as much as audience.

- Choose a Disney film that you know well (e.g., *Cinderella, Mulan, Beauty and the Beast*). What are some of the key characteristics of the film? What ideas or messages are being represented? How? What evidence do you have (or would you need to research) to support your thesis?

Analyzing Historical Relevance. Read words and images closely for a rhetorical analysis that focuses on historical relevance.

- Watch a music video that uses historical footage. Find five pieces of factual information about that historical context. Discuss how the video's footage manages to (or fails to) relate to the song. Start with a two-sentence summary of the video. Follow the summary with a working thesis statement. What points do you want to make? How will factual information help you develop your points?

Activity: Planning and Organizing the Text Analysis Essay

Even though you may choose another pattern of organization for your essay, it's helpful to begin with a basic plan as you gather your evidence and anticipate your audience's needs and questions. This working outline is adapted from *Easy Writer.*

I. **Introduction**

- *Summarize* your text as concisely as possible (try to do this in three lines or less if you can).

  _____

  _____

  _____

  _____

  _____

  _____

- Provide your *thesis statement* by the end of paragraph 1. Write it out here.

  _____

  _____

  _____

  _____

  _____

  _____

II. **Background.** What do readers need to know to understand this text and your thesis? List that information here and *note your sources*. You will want to keep a collection of your sources for when you compile your Works Cited page at the end.

_____

_____

_____

_____

_____

III. **Lines of Argument**

- Reason #1. State the first point you want to prove about your text. What evidence can you provide from your text or your research?

_____

_____

_____

_____

_____

_____

- Reason #2. State your next point. What evidence can you provide?

_____

_____

_____

_____

_____

_____

- Reason #3 _and so on_. Continue to assert your points clearly and back them with evidence. Make sure that each point ties back to the thesis statement you established on page 1.

_____

_____

_____

_____

_____

_____

IV. **Conclusion.** As you bring your analysis to a conclusion, you have several strategies to consider. Here are some you may want to adopt: (1) Elaborate on implications of your thesis statement. (2) Make clear what you want readers to think. (3) Make a strong ethical or emotional appeal in a memorable way. (4) Evaluate the text's effectiveness for its audience. (5) Evaluate the text's effectiveness for yourself. (You are also welcome to create a concluding strategy of your own.)

WRITING A THESIS STATEMENT

A thesis is a statement that clearly explains an author's main idea for a piece of writing (Lunsford 371). Thesis statements are actually a convention of many academic essays. They are typical in genres like research papers, editorials, and even books, but less common in narratives and profiles.

For your text analysis essay, you will need a thesis for your paper. Here's a quick two-step process for drafting a tentative thesis. Remember, it's hard to write a thesis until you do research. It's also okay for your thesis to change depending on what sort of information you uncover while you're writing.

Step One: Write the Question You Are Trying to Answer

Often your instructor (in English 101 and other courses) will give you a question, but even if they don't you should try to identify one. Here's a possible example for the analysis paper.

> How does this advertisement for the Humane Society try to persuade its audience to donate?

Once you have a question, you are halfway to having a thesis. Also note, just as your thesis can change, you may find that you need to change your question too. It all depends on what you uncover through your research and writing.

Step Two: Write an Answer to Your Question Using the Same Language

Use the language from your question to write an answer, even if it's just a guess at this point.

> The advertisement for the Humane Society tries to persuade its audience to donate by evoking emotions like sympathy through images of starving or abused animals and by telling the audience how even small amounts of money can have lasting effects.

There you have it. You can always change what you've written but having a clear thesis will help your audience see your main point, and it can even help you clarify what it is you're trying to say.

Myths and Facts about Thesis Statements

There are a lot of myths and facts about thesis statements. It's important to know the difference. Here are a few to discuss as a class.

Fact: Thesis statements include a topic and a comment on the topic.

Myth: Thesis statements can only be one sentence long.

Fact: The best thesis statements are debatable.

Myth: Thesis statements must present one claim supported by three ideas.

Fact: Thesis statements will often appear at the end of the first paragraph of an academic essay.

Workshop: Peer Review
for the Rhetorical Analysis

Author: _____

Title: _____

Reader: _____

INTRODUCTION (base your responses just on the first paragraph for this section)

What text is the essay about? _____
_____
_____
_____

What is the main idea of the essay? _____
_____
_____
_____

What could the author do to make that main idea even clearer? _____
_____
_____
_____
_____
_____
_____

AUDIENCE

Who does the author describe as the audience of this text? _____

Do you think this has changed over time? If so, explain how.

_____
_____
_____
_____
_____

Were there any historically significant events that contributed to the text, its audience, and the interpretation? Describe how this works or does not work in the essay.

_____

_____

_____

_____

_____

THE TEXT ITSELF

How frequently is the actual text referred to in a specific way?

_____

_____

_____

_____

_____

Are there instances where rhetorical appeals are referenced to explain how the text works? Y/N

Make at least one suggestion to improve this section.

_____

_____

_____

_____

_____

Finally, comment about the use of citations and Works Cited. Are they correct? If not, remind them of what they are missing.

_____

_____

_____

_____

_____

Reflective Cover Memo

Date: _____

To (Instructor's Name): _____

From (Author of Paper): _____

Subject: _____

Reflective Cover Memo for "Final for Now"—Text Analysis

Writing Process. Please reflect on your writing process. What did you try for the first time? What comments from peer workshop and conferences did you explore in your revision? How did this improve your paper? Please cite concrete examples.

_____

_____

_____

_____

_____

_____

Analysis. What is your thesis statement/argument? What evidence did you use to support your overall argument? List the major points of your analysis in skeleton form. Now, briefly reflect on how effectively you think you put this analysis together and communicated it.

_____

_____

_____

_____

_____

_____

How did you discuss the author, audience, and the text itself? How was your analysis original? What unique things do you think you had to say about this text?

_____

_____

_____

_____

_____

_____

Future Writing. What plans do you have for revisions of this paper for the final portfolio draft?

_____

_____

_____

_____

_____

Questions or Comments. What questions do you have for your instructor about the construction of your paper or the writing process? What would you like your instructor to focus on while reading the "Final for Now" version of this paper?

_____

_____

_____

_____

_____

Using this Piece in English 101. What do you want English 101 students and teachers to know about this piece of writing? How do you want them to use this text in classrooms?

_____

_____

_____

_____

_____

_____

_____

Reflective Cover Memo

Date: 1 February 2018

To (Instructor's Name): English 101 Instructors and Students

From (Author of Paper): Meredith Jeffers

Subject: Reflection on "Final for Now" Version of Is Logging the Answer to West Virginia's State Park Problem?

Reflective Cover Memo for "Final for Now"—Text Analysis

Writing Process. Please reflect on your writing process. What did you try for the first time? What comments from peer workshop and conferences did you explore in your revision? How did this improve your paper? Please cite concrete examples.

This was my first time writing a text analysis, and I tried to use what we've learned in class about rhetoric throughout my paper. I have never analyzed something with ethos, logos, and pathos before, so that was a new experience for me. Sometimes I felt confused about the difference between the three, but my classmates helped me figure it out during peer review.

Analysis. What is your thesis statement/argument? What evidence did you use to support your overall argument? List the major points of your analysis in skeleton form. Now, briefly reflect on how effectively you think you put this analysis together and communicated it.

I analyzed the "Save Our State Parks" article to see whether or not it is persuasive at arguing against SB 270. I think it is persuasive because it shows that logging would hurt tourism and not actually make that much money.

How did you discuss the author, audience, and the text itself? How was your analysis original? What unique things do you think you had to say about this text?

I think that my analysis is original because I also live in West Virginia and know how beautiful the state is, so it is upsetting to think that the state parks could suffer from this bill. The West Virginia Rivers Coalition is an activist group so it was maybe a bit biased, but they did a good job arguing their points.

Future Writing. What plans do you have for revisions of this paper for the final portfolio draft?

I think I want to make this paper longer for the final portfolio. I had a hard time reaching the word count without feeling like I was repeating myself.

Questions or Comments. What questions do you have for your instructor about the construction of your paper or the writing process? What would you like your instructor to focus on while reading the "Final for Now" version of this paper?

Did I do a good job talking about rhetoric? I feel like I couldn't find some of the strategies we talked about in class, like constraints, but I don't know if that's because there aren't any or if I don't know where to look for them.

Using this Piece in English 101. What do you want English 101 students and teachers to know about this piece of writing? How do you want them to use this text in classrooms?

This is not a flawless text analysis, but that is also not the point. It would be most beneficial to identify the strengths and weaknesses of the essay, and to address how those weaknesses could be revised in the next draft for the final portfolio. Pay particular attention to how this paper analyzes audience and purpose based on what you learned in the "Exploring and Analyzing Texts" activity in this chapter. How effectively does this paper address audience and purpose? What question is this paper's thesis statement attempting to answer? How can the thesis be clearer and more effective? What rhetorical strategies does this paper analyze, and does it do so effectively?

SAMPLE ANALYSIS

Meredith Jeffers   Jeffers   1

Professor Sura

English 101

1 February 2018

Is Logging the Answer to West Virginia's State Park Problem?

West Virginia: Wild and Wonderful, the Mountain State, Almost Heaven. These nicknames all have one thing in common: they speak to the beauty of West Virginia's landscape. Visit any of West Virginia's beautiful state parks, and it is easy to see why the state would be so proud of its natural beauty. However, West Virginia's state parks are hurting financially, and, because of these massive debts, a new bill has been introduced that will raise revenue. If passed, Senate Bill 270 (or SB 270) will allow logging in state parks. Many conservation groups oppose SB 270 based on its environmental destructiveness. One such group is the West Virginia Rivers Coalition. In their article titled "Save Our State Parks," the WV Rivers Coalition effectively argues against SB 270 by appealing to its audience through ethos, pathos, and logos.

To better understand SB 270, it is first necessary to understand the background of the situation. The West Virginia state park system currently faces a "$50 million maintenance backlog," and it needs to find revenue in order to pay it back (Public Lands). In 2017, the West Virginia Division of Natural Resources (DNR) planned to charge admission fees to seven West Virginia state parks and forests: Babcock State Park, Blackwater Falls State Park, Cacapon Resort State Park, Coopers Rock State Forest, Little Beaver State Park, Pipestem Resort State Park, and Valley Falls State Park. The DNR Director, Stephen McDaniel, said, "The goal is to reduce the gap between expenditures and revenue." The DNR planned to offer two passes, "an annual pass with unlimited entrance to the parks for $12 per vehicle or a single-day vehicle pass for $2," with the money collected at each park going directly

back to that park. This plan was supposed to "generate an additional $1 million to

$1.2 million annually" (Pace). However, the DNR's admissions fee plan was canceled

by West Virginia Governor Jim Justice on April 26, 2017. He said that it was a "bad

idea" because "West Virginians are struggling," and he did not believe it was fair

to charge fees (Binns). This still left major questions: how could West Virginia state

parks pay back its debts?

All of this information is important to understand the context of the situa-

tion. In "Backpacks vs. Briefcases: Steps toward Rhetorical Analysis," Laura Bolin

Carroll defines context by saying that "[rhetorical] messages always occur in a

specific situation or context," and that context is divided into three parts: exigence,

audience, and constraints (Carroll 48). In the article from WV Rivers Coalition, the

exigence, or the thing the article is responding to, is the introduction of SB 270. The

audience is people in West Virginia, people who care about the environment, and

anyone who uses state parks. Constraints are like limits. In this case, it is unclear

what the constraints are. Now that we understand the context, we can look at the

article and see if it is effective or ineffective in arguing against SB 270.

The "Save Our State Parks" article starts by introducing the issue of West Vir-

ginia state parks needing revenue and providing background on SB 270. The stance

of the article and what it is arguing for is clear from the beginning because it says that

"groups across the state are united in an effort to oppose SB 270 and any commercial

logging in West Virginia State Parks." From the outset, you know that this article is

going to be giving reasons about why SB 270 is a bad idea. Do they present those

reasons persuasively, though?

Jeffers   3

One way that the article tries to reach its audience is through ethos, pathos, and logos. Carroll defines ethos as "credibility," which means, can the audience believe the message? The WV River Coalition is definitely credible. On their website, they talk about being a non-profit organization, so you know that they are doing this because they love it and not because it will make them a lot of money. The organization is also over 20 years old, so they have been doing this a long time. This makes them more credible than a brand-new organization because they've had time to establish themselves as activists in West Virginia. Because of their history and work in West Virginia, it makes their message especially believable because they are experts on the topic, so we should listen to what they say.

The article uses pathos to persuade the audience that SB 270 is a bad idea. Like I said in my introduction, West Virginia has many nicknames that have to do with nature. One of them, Almost Heaven, comes from John Denver's song "Take Me Home, Country Roads." Basically everyone at WVU has heard this song, especially if they've been to a football game. "Almost Heaven" is a phrase to be proud of, and many West Virginians (and temporary West Virginians) are. In the article, the WV Rivers Coalitions appeals to this sense of pride by suggesting that the passage of SB 270 will hurt West Virginia and its landscape, and make it harder for us to be proud in the state.

One of the reasons the article provides for why SB 270 shouldn't be passed is because it will cause "[damage] to the Wild and Wonderful brand." This brand is key to West Virginia's tourism campaign, which they argue will be hurt by SB 270 because "the 'Wild and Wonderful' forests of our state parks... are our natural competitive advantage in the tourism market." If we allow logging, then the forests will be damaged, which might impact whether or not people decide to visit West Virginia on their vacations.

Jeffers   4

Perhaps the most effective way that this article argues against SB 270 is through its use of logos, or an appeal to logic. Logos are typically associated with statistics and numbers, or other facts rooted in hard evidence. The WV Rivers Coalition provides numerous facts about why logging will actually hurt West Virginia instead of helping it. For example, they say that "logging our state parks could actually lower the price of timber" because SB 270 is a commitment to a 20-year bond that will help repay the park system's debt. To prove their point, they reference that "average timber prices [dropped] by a third between 2014–2016." With such recent data suggesting that logging is, at best, an unpredictable industry that might not even pay off financially for the park system. Also, they argue that SB 270 could put the federal funding that the parks receive at risk. The Land and Water Conservation Fund "has given over $7 million to WV for acquisition and upkeep of state parks," so allowing logging would go directly against this mission and keep WV from getting more grants in the future. The WV Rivers Coalition also uses logos to argue about the great things about the state parks, too. For example, in 2015 the state parks "contributed to $230 million West Virginia's economy." This shows that audience that the state parks are a good investment for West Virginia because they end up making so much revenue.

In conclusion, the message that the WV Rivers Coalition argues is clear: SB 270 will only end up hurting West Virginia financially and environmentally. They argue this message well by showing strong ethos, pathos, and logos. If West Virginia wants to attract tourists, generate more money, and not ruin the beauty of the natural landscape, then they should not pass SB 270.

Jeffers 5

Works Cited

Binns, Brooke. "State park fee repealed by governor." *The Inter-Mountain* 26 April 2017.

Carroll, Laura Bolin. "Backpacks vs. Briefcases: Steps toward Rhetorical Analysis."

Writing Spaces: Readings on Writing, Parlor Press, 2001.

Pace, Fred. "7 WV state parks to require entrance fees." *The Herald-Dispatch* 26 April 2017.

"Save Our State Parks." *West Virginia Rivers*, http://wvrivers.org/2018/01/sosparks.

Accessed 1. February 2018.

"Save Our State Parks Alternative Revenue." *West Virginia Rivers*, http://wvrivers.

org/2018/01/sosparksrevenue. Accessed 1 February 2018.

There Are Two Sides (or more) to Every Story

Chapter 6 is the last major project of the course prior to the portfolio. In this unit you will analyze an issue by researching the different people who have a stake in it. You'll also examine what it means to let your research guide your thesis.

GETTING STARTED

Overview of Project: Writing to Explain Multiple Perspectives

PURPOSE

You've probably heard the expression, "There are two sides to every story." The purpose of this assignment is to use what you've learned about telling stories, collecting information, and conducting analysis in order to explain not just two but multiple sides to a complex issue.

AUDIENCE

Your instructor may have specific instructions about what audience to write for. Otherwise, consider writing for an audience of people invested in the issue you are discussing. Be mindful of how people with differing ideas would react to your writing. Don't just write for the people who agree with you. Try not to alienate the people who don't agree with you. Ask yourself, "How can I get the people who disagree on this issue to listen to what I'm saying?"

CONVENTIONS

The genre for this chapter is the exploratory essay. In an exploratory essay, you start with a central question or tentative idea. Then you conduct research to learn more about that question or idea. Finally, you explain what you learned through your exploration.

TROUBLE SPOTS

You've probably realized by now that there are almost always options for organizing a piece of writing. As a writer, you have to think critically about what information should come first, what should come second, and so on. You'll have to do that again here but remember what you've learned about introductions, conclusions, Works Cited pages, and MLA format.

In addition, because this paper asks you to explain multiple perspectives, you'll need to consider a range of people who have a stake in your issue (i.e., stakeholders) and find information that will help you explain their points of view. It is important to remember to acknowledge all points of view, including those that disagree with yours.

ASSESSMENT

Your instructor may adjust the criteria below to fit the specific project for your course. In any case, here are a few key criteria to keep in mind:

- This paper will focus on one meaningful issue.

- This paper will include a clear tentative thesis or research question at the beginning of your essay.

- This paper will demonstrate information that helps you explain multiple perspectives.

- This paper will integrate sources effectively with appropriate citations.

- This paper will organize your argument in a way that makes a difficult issue easy to understand.

- This paper will use an engaging voice that draws in readers with diverse points of view.

- This paper will produce approximately 1,500 to 1,750 words (5–6 pages) of polished writing.

Exploring Ideas

In many cases, the choice of topic for this unit is up to you although your instructor may have a theme to help you focus your ideas.

One way to get started on a project is to complete a freewrite about a topic of interest to you. Take a look at the three topics listed below:

- Social Media

- Free College Tuition

- Food on Campus

Just for practice, pick one of these topics and complete a freewrite on it.

> Remember, a freewrite is a short, timed writing exercise. You should not stop writing, and you should not worry about grammar or punctuation. Just get your ideas onto the page.

Try it now. For the next two minutes, write down everything you know, think you know, or want to know about one of these topics. Do it right here in the book.

On your mark. Get set. Go!

_____

_____

_____

_____

_____

_____

_____

_____

_____

_____

_____

_____

_____

_____

_____

_____

_____

_____

Activity: Creating a Plan for the Exploratory Essay

Date: _____

To: _____

From: _____

Subject: A Working Plan for the Exploratory Essay

Please fill in the sections below to provide a reader with a clear sense of your working plan for this paper.

Research Question. What issue have you selected? Try to phrase a key question or two that your project will address. Have you made sure that your research represents more than one perspective on the issue? Make sure to explain the multiple points of view that surround your topic.

_____

_____

_____

_____

_____

_____

Research Plans. What articles, books, or other texts have you found, or when do you plan to do some library research? Whom might you interview, survey, or ask for direction?

_____

_____

_____

_____

_____

_____

Main Idea and Purpose. What seems to be the main idea and focus of the whole project? What seems to be the purpose? How are you sure that you have a focus that is specific enough to allow you to say something unique?

_____

_____

_____

_____

_____

_____

DOES THIS PAPER HAVE A THESIS?

Since thesis statements appeared in the last chapter, we want to address them again here because exploratory essays may ask you do something different than what you're used to regarding thesis statements.

> Recall that a thesis is a statement that clearly explains an author's main idea for a piece of writing (Lunsford 371) and that thesis statements are conventions of many academic essays.

For your "Writing to Explain Multiple Perspectives" essay, you want to focus on allowing your thesis to develop as you research difference perspectives and stakeholders. In other words, you shouldn't pick a position on an issue and then try to prove it.

Instead, you want to start with a **working thesis** that describes what you think the answer to your research question is. Then as you explore the issue by doing research on different perspectives and stakeholders, you may find your thesis growing, changing, and developing. That's a good thing.

For this reason, your instructor may ask you to put your working thesis or research question in the introduction and then your revised (or final) thesis at the conclusion in order to mark the end of your exploration of the issue. In other words, you still have a thesis, it's just located in a different place because you're writing in a difference genre.

On the other hand, your instructor may still ask you to place your thesis at the end of the first paragraph of your essay. Then, the rest of your paper will support and explain that thesis by using your research.

Either way is fine. Just remember: You can't really write your thesis until you do your research.

Activity: Audience and the Exploratory Essay

Now that you have a topic, have a research question, and have had time to do a little research, how will you frame a thesis to reach an audience that includes more than one stakeholder (including some readers who may disagree with your view)?

Some things to think about:

- What rhetorical claims and appeals might you make to your audience?

- Where will you start?

- How will you anticipate questions or opposition?

- Where will you integrate research to provide support for your argument?

If your topic is, for instance, wind power, here's how you might begin:

1. You've narrowed the topic to look at the issue locally:

   Wind power and its effect on West Virginians.

2. Who are some stakeholders? (Be sure that you have chosen stakeholders who represent a broad range of perspectives on the issue.)

   Politicians, local residents, environmental activists, and state tourism advocates.

3. Once you have chosen four stakeholders, think about what perspective each represents.

   For example, would state tourism advocates see the issue in economic terms?

4. Which stakeholders will be your primary readers? Who else might you persuade? What evidence will you need to support your position?

   For instance, if you want to persuade politicians to support wind power, how might you argue for cleaner energy options using emissions data?

   Are there economic advantages you might also cite?

   What opposition might you anticipate?

5. Think about the stance you want to take, the readers you want to persuade, the ways you'll use your research to make your case, and the type of rhetorical strategies and appeals that might be useful. Fill out the chart below to help you organize your ideas.

	WHY IS THEIR PERSPECTIVE INTERESTING AND IMPORTANT?	WHAT RESEARCH DO YOU NEED TO DO TO UNDERSTAND AND ACKNOWLEDGE THEIR PERSPECTIVE?	WHAT RHETORICAL STRATEGIES MIGHT APPEAL TO THIS READER—AND WHY?
STAKEHOLDER 1			
STAKEHOLDER 2			
STAKEHOLDER 3			
STAKEHOLDER 4			

USING WVU LIBRARIES ONLINE

What are LibGuides? LibGuides are websites created by WVU librarians to help students and researchers find course or topic-specific resources in one place. For instance, you can find WVU LibGuides on folklore, African-American history, interior design, psychology, and much more.

How can the English 101 LibGuide help you? The English 101 LibGuide offers a single place from which you can do all of your research. You can get ideas about potential topics; use Library databases to find journal, magazine, and newspaper articles; search the Libraries' online catalog for books; and even chat online with a librarian if you need help.

Use the 101 LibGuide to find topics for any of your papers using CQ Researcher. Find relevant newspaper or magazine coverage of an issue for your profile using the LexisNexis search. Find scholarly articles for your Text Analysis or Exploratory essays using Academic Search Premier. If you ever get stuck, check out the tutorials or contact a librarian via chat or e-mail.

How do you get there? The WVU LibGuides' home is located at *http://libguides. wvu.edu*.

- At the WVU LibGuides' homepage, find the left-hand menu, **Browse by Subjects**. As you can see, we have LibGuides for many different subjects.

- Choose **English**. You'll then be taken to a page with all of the LibGuides for English.

- Click on the link **English 101 Research Guide** (*http://libguides.wvu.edu/english101*).

USING CQ RESEARCHER

For the Exploratory Essay, it is important to find a topic, and then narrow this topic down so that you can create a manageable and unique research question. Then, you also need to do research to better understand who the stakeholders are for your issue. Finally, you need to find research to explore the positions of each of your stakeholders. CQ Researcher is a great place to start this work.

- From the Library home page, select the Databases tab and type **CQ Researcher** into the search bar.

- Then click on the link that says **CQ Researcher**.

Searching CQ Researcher

There are two ways that you can search CQ Researcher: either by **Browse Topic** (best if you have a broad topic that you want to research and need to narrow it down) and **Quick Search** (best if you have a narrow topic and keywords already).

BROWSE TOPIC

- Check out the demo video at the English 101 LibGuides; it's under the Getting Started tab. It will show you how to use the Browse Topic link to find good focused research questions and walk you through a report's features.

- Look at the recent reports on CQ Researcher or look through the list of topics, and try to find a topic that interests you. Then, when you browse the report for this topic, you can begin to narrow your topic down and create your own research question.

QUICK SEARCH

- If you have a focused research question already, list your keywords and use the **Quick Search** box to find reports.

Using a CQ Researcher Report

CQ Reports all have the following sections: Introduction; Overview; "The Issues" Subheadings; Background; Current Situation; Outlook; Pro/Con; Chronology; Short Features; Footnotes/Bibliography; Contacts; About the Author; Document Citation.

Let's examine the CQ report *Middle Class Squeeze: Is More Government Aid Needed?* (6 March 2009) to see how you can use a report to find a research question, determine stakeholders, and do some added research. [Go to *CQ Researcher* on Libraries' Databases page (*http://www.libraries.wvu.edu/databases/*) to see this report; CQ is listed under C.]

The **Subheadings** on the issues surrounding the topic often make good focused research questions and let you know who is affected by a particular issue—who the stakeholders are. The sections *Is a stable middle class a thing of the past?; Is overconsumption at the root of the middle class' problems?; Are aggressive new government programs needed to bolster the middle class?* all would make excellent focused research questions. Further, these questions identify stakeholders: legislators, members of the middle class, people who market to middle-class consumers, banks who loan to the middle class, employers of middle class workers, and so on.

The **Short Features** section usually discusses side issues to the topic at hand and can offer more potential research questions. For example, both *What Does 'Middle Class' Really Mean?* and *Economic Meltdown Batters Retirement Plans: Reform proposals call for limiting risk to workers* would make good focuses for research papers and allow you to see more stakeholders in an issue, including people who expect to retire in the next few years, the recently unemployed, investment bankers, and so on.

The **Pro/Con** section presents two essays, each arguing one side of an issue. The Pro/Con essay for *Middle Class Squeeze* asks *Has U.S. trade and globalization policy hurt the middle class?* This would make yet another focused way to examine the broader issue of middle-class economic woes. Those arguing the two sides can be seen as stakeholders themselves and as authorities on these issues. Remember, a good paper will examine the many sides of an issue.

Don't forget to use the **Bibliography** and **Footnotes** section to get started on research; many of the sources are linked to online full-text articles.

HOW TO USE THE POINTS OF VIEW REFERENCE CENTER DATABASE

Points of View is a free database made available to students at WVU through the library's website. This is a useful database for the Exploratory Essay because it gathers a variety of opinions and perspectives on issues.

The easiest way to get to this database is to head to the The WVU English 101 Research LibGuide, located at *http://libguides.wvu.edu/english101*

Simply scroll down the main page, and it is the second search engine listed.

This is the homepage of the database:

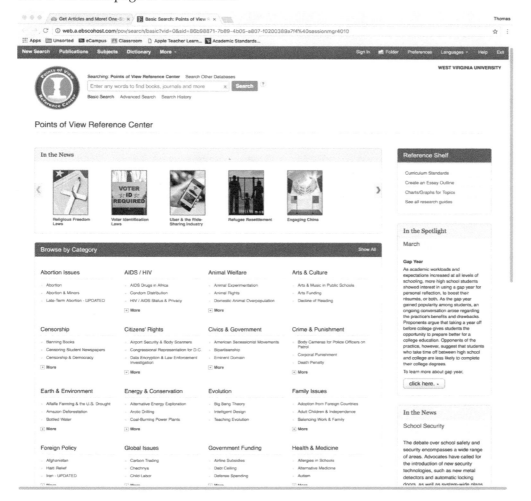

1. **Quick Links** (located on the bottom half of the homepage) allows people who may not have a topic in mind to browse by category or by broad categories. You can then look for subcategories to narrow your topic down. For example, "Global Issues" contains topics like "Carbon Trading," "Third World Relief," "Nuclear Proliferation," and others. You can also find a narrower topic by scrolling through a larger list of all individual topics sorted alphabetically.

2. **Research Guides** (located in the upper right-hand corner of the homepage) offers you links to articles with advice on how to choose a topic for your paper and what to do if your topic seems too narrow or too broad, how to create an essay outline from your research notes, how to cite sources, and many other resources.

3. **Search** allows people who have a topic in mind to input their own topics of interest and locate corresponding articles and images. What makes this database unique is that it sorts its findings under a number of tabs (All Results, Points of View, Periodicals, Newspapers, etc.). The default is "Points of View," so you will want to check out the other tabs or click on "All Results" to see the rest of the available resources. (For example, a quick search for "Strip Mining" returns four "Points of View" articles.)

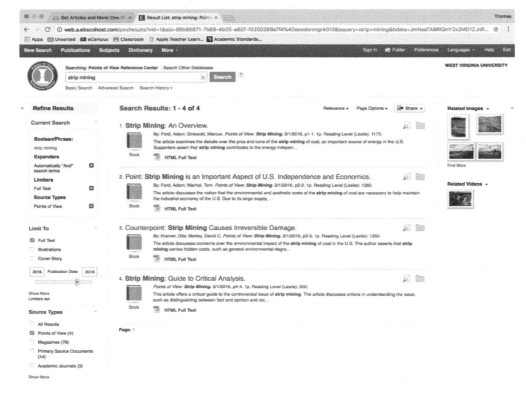

When you click on "Magazine," the number of search results jumps from 4 to 83.

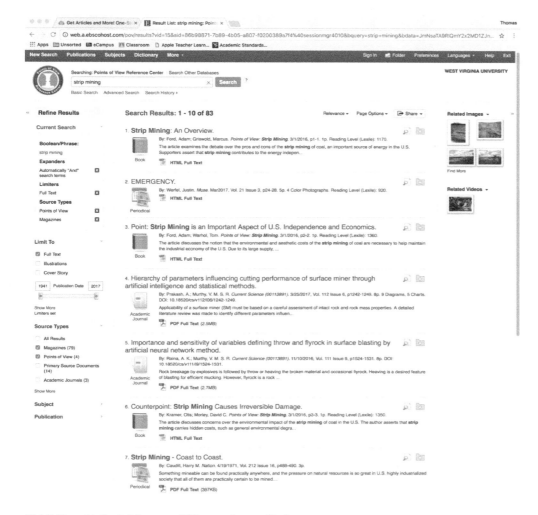

("All Results" yields over 500 search results.)

Advanced Search Options allows you to limit your search by document type and publication date. This also allows you to search only for PDF Full Text articles and Peer Reviewed articles. This may be useful depending on your requirements for the papers.

NOTES

When you find articles you are interested in, you can add them to a folder for easy retrieval later, download them, or print them off. If you like a particular article, you can click on the link at the left of the page, "Find Similar Results," and it will take you to similar articles.

Workshop: Peer Review for the Exploratory Essay

Author:_____

Title: _____

Reader:_____

Writers: What type of response would be most useful to you at this stage in your writing?

Readers: As you read, please write down your answers to the questions the writer has identified. As usual, go ahead and write directly on the draft you're reading, and *please remember to sign your comments*.

1. Please read the draft through once for an **INITIAL RESPONSE**.

    *   What was your **first impression** of the paper as a whole?

    *   What **reaction** did it leave you with?

2. Please read through the paper for **FOCUS AND AUDIENCE**.

    *   What is the **main idea and focus** of the draft? Please mark the place in the paper where the main idea comes across.

    *   Does the main idea need to be clarified or focused further? Does the main idea need to be introduced sooner?

    *   Who seems to be the **audience** for this paper? How can you tell? What might help reach the intended audience? Can you suggest an alternative audience?

3. Please read the paper to look at **EVIDENCE AND DOCUMENTATION.**

    *   Where does the writer offer **evidence** beyond his/her own experience?

    *   How does the writer introduce the evidence?

    *   When passages or examples are cited, does the writer explain how and why they're significant? Do the examples continually relate back to the main idea?

    *   Are sources fully acknowledged? Check the in-text citations and Works Cited for accuracy.

    *   Identify at least one place where you need more evidence or more explanation.

4. Please read the paper to look at **ORGANIZATION**.

    *   How does the writer group information and signal transitions to help the essay cohere?

    *   **Try a sentence outline, OR a list of possible section headings, OR a traditional outline, OR a flowchart to look at the organization. Suggest one way the writer might develop the topic.**

    *   Suggest anything else that would improve the organization or development of the paper.

Activity: Reverse Outlining to Check Organization

One common strategy of organization is called **reverse outlining**. The "reverse" here indicates that this tactic is used after you've written an initial draft, or at least most of one. You then create an outline of what you've written. This lets you (or a reader) take a step back from the draft to evaluate the strengths and weaknesses of the organization and the argument itself.

1. **Reread the draft carefully.**

   Read your paper over, and as you do so, identify the thesis, and then make very brief notes in the margin about what each paragraph is trying to say and do. Essentially, you are meant to be tracking the ideas in your paper as they collectively build toward a persuasive argument (which is ideally captured in your thesis statement).

2. **Outline the draft.**

   After you've read through the entire essay, transfer the brief notes into a list in the order they appear in the essay. The goal is to say not only *what* each paragraph says but also *how* it advances the argument.

   Para 1 tries to (*Introduce the topic? Capture the reader's attention? Both? How?*)

   _____

   Para 2 tries to _____

   Para 3 _____

   Para 4 _____

   Para 5 _____

   Para 6 _____

   Para 7 _____

   Para 8 _____

   Para 9 _____

   Para 10 _____

   Para 11 _____

   Para 12 _____

   And so on (using the reverse side or another piece of paper if needed).

3. **Examine the thesis, the outline, and the draft together.**

   Look closely at the outline and see how it holds up as a model for demonstrating the validity of the thesis statement. You should be able to determine which paragraphs need to be better connected, if they are in a logical order, and if any are irrelevant to the focus of your argument.

Reflective Cover Memo

Date: _____

To (Instructor's Name): _____

From (Author of Paper): _____

Subject: _____

Reflective Cover Memo for "Final for Now"—Exploratory Essay

Writing Process. Please reflect on your writing process. What worked? What did you try for the first time? Did you take any risks? What are you most proud of? Anything you found challenging? What else should I know about how this paper evolved?

_____

_____

_____

_____

_____

_____

Changes and Revisions. What changed between your initial research question and the "Final for Now" version? Why?

_____

_____

_____

_____

_____

_____

Analyzing Your Own Writing. Perform a very brief rhetorical analysis of your own paper. What are the dominant rhetorical strategies and appeals that you used to make your argument persuasive to your audience?

_____

_____

_____

_____

_____

_____

_____

Future Writing. What else might you have discussed in this paper if you had more time/space? What plans do you have for revisions of this paper for the final portfolio?

_____

_____

_____

_____

_____

Questions or Comments. Is there anything you'd like your instructor to keep in mind when reading the "Final for Now" version of this paper?

_____

_____

_____

_____

_____

Using this Piece in English 101. What do you want English 101 students and teachers to know about this piece of writing? How do you want them to use this text in classrooms?

_____

_____

_____

_____

_____

Reflective Cover Memo

Date: November 25, 2017

To: English 101 Instructors and Students

From: Katie Vogelpohl

Subject: Reflection on "Final for Now" Version of Expanding the Viewpoint of the National Park Service

Reflective Cover Memo for "Final for Now"—Exploratory Essay

Writing Process. Please reflect on your writing process. What worked? What did you try for the first time? Did you take any risks? What are you most proud of? Anything you found challenging? What else should I know about how this paper evolved?

I think that I did a nice job of finding sources that worked to support my argument. I like the articles that I read, and I think they all are credible and clear.

One thing that I struggled with was the evolution of my thesis. I believed in my topic from the start, so I don't really know how much my thesis changed with time. Maybe I haven't started to look at all of the POVs yet. I feel like there is someone that I could be missing.

Changes and Revisions. What changed between your initial research question and the "Final for Now" version? Why?

Initially, I just wanted to know how the National Parks Service was helping the American people, but I ended up talking more about how the National Parks Service could end to reach even more people. While the parks service is super popular now, they are missing a huge market. They even say themselves that they are not super diverse.

I realized how the parks service could change early in the process, so even though my thinking changed, I am worried that I don't demonstrate that change going through my paper.

Analyzing Your Own Writing. Perform a very brief rhetorical analysis of your own paper. What are the dominant rhetorical strategies and appeals that you used to make your argument persuasive to your audience?

I rely most heavily on logos and pathos in my paper. I use multiple facts and statistics to support what I am saying about the parks service. I also use pathos, discussing both the importance of the parks for the future generations and the effect that non-diverse park structures are having on impoverished areas and non-white populations.

Future Writing. What else might you have discussed in this paper if you had more time/space? What plans do you have for revisions of this paper for the final portfolio?

I brought up, but didn't really talk about, how the parks service could be looking into technology advancements. I think that there is a lot that the parks could be doing, both in terms of looking into technology history and technology itself. I mean, most parks are pretty "rustic" and "outdated." It could be interesting to look into if there are any "high tech" parks, and what they do. If not, maybe we need some.

Questions or Comments. Is there anything you'd like your instructor to keep in mind while reading the "Final for Now" version of this paper?

It would be helpful for me if you were able to tell me if I am doing a decent job of showing the multiple stakes in the paper. I can see them, since I talk about diverse populations, the parks service itself, and local economies, but maybe they aren't as clear as I like.

Also, does my thesis change enough to show development from the beginning to the end? Or does it need to be such a dramatic change that it can't be missed? I don't think that I am going to reverse my view on this topic, so how would my thesis really change?

Using this Piece in English 101. What do you want English 101 students and teachers to know about this piece of writing? How do you want them to use this text in classrooms?

Using this piece in the classroom, the instructor could take the time to discuss some of the strengths of the paper, such as the integration of quotes and research or some of the potential weaknesses, such as the general organization. This paper leaves the paragraph that best addresses multiple stakeholders until the end. Is that a good idea, or would this paper benefit from discussing the multiple viewpoints throughout? Why or why not? I also recommend using this paper as a source to search out weak wording that could be replaced by clearer or stronger statements. This paper could also present that opportunity to discuss the value of credible sources. Are all of these sources strong? How can you tell if a source is strong or weak? What could the writer have done better to emphasize the strength or credibility of the sources?

SAMPLE EXPLORATORY ESSAY

Katie Vogelpohl   Vogelpohl   1

Professor Sura

ENGL 101

November 25, 2017

Expanding the Viewpoint of the National Park Service

In 2016, the United State's National Park Service celebrated its centennial anniversary with parks around the country hosting thousands of public programs and events throughout the year. Among these programs were Urban Agenda, which organized city parks to promote their relevance to locals; Every Kid in a Park, which offered all fourth graders free admission to the parks to encourage a connection with the younger generation; and the NPS Centennial Act, which was designed to look for new ways that the parks could grow in the next 100 years (Centennial Initiatives). In 2015, the parks had record attendance numbers over 300 million, and the National Parks Service (NPS) is hoping to keep that number on the rise (Flowers). As the NPS looks forward into possible areas of growth for the future, it is important to consider how the parks can better work with currently underrepresented historical moments, such as major scientific advancements, latino history, and notable women in history. By expanding the focus of the National Park Service, the parks could shed light on previously ignored historical figures while also increasing visitation numbers and improving local and national economies.

By and large, most of the U.S. National Parks are dedicated to either natural wonders or historical accomplishments by white males. Despite comprising more than half of the population, of the current 410 U.S. national park sites, only eight are dedicated to an aspect of women's history (Errick). Further, 54 million Hispanics and Latinos reside in the United States, yet less than 1% of historical landmarks and only 4% of national parks are dedicated to the Latino communities (Thakar and Magana).

Vogelpohl   2

In 2013, the NPS' Office of Relevancy, Diversity, and Inclusion was developed in or-der to "address the lack of people of color in national parks" (Root). This group was initially devised with the priority of increasing the number of non-white visitors and employees in the parks, as a late 2009 service of the parks noted that 78% of visitors that year were white, while only 9% were Hispanic, and 7% were African American (Root). However, as the lack of diversity in the parks has clearly been noted by the system itself, it raises the question as to why more parks are not being designed to honor and celebrate a broader variety of cultures and accomplishments.

Former associate director for workforce and inclusion at NPS, Michael Reyn-olds, has acknowledged that, "we [the National Park Service] have a definite diver-sity issue." Current head of the Office of Relevancy, Diversity and Inclusion, Sangita Chari, echoes this sentiment, explaining that many non-white individuals are choos-ing not to come to the parks because "we haven't become relevant to them in their life." (Root). Yet, it can be assumed that with a more variety in the topics and interests of the park system, there would be an increase in the number of diverse visitors. The success of the few current urban and historical sites dedicated to men and women of color, such as the Harriet Tubman Underground Railroad and the Charles Young Buffalo Soldiers National Monument are already demonstrating how more diverse topics encourage an influx in all visitors, including visitors of color. By dedicating the parks to a broader range of cultural groups and more recent, though historically significant topics, the parks could expect even more visitors, including individuals who previously believed the parks to be irrelevant to their lives.

Increasing the range of offerings in the parks would not simply improve the number of diverse visitors, but may work to increase the overall success of the park system throughout the year. Currently, the most popular national parks in the coun-

NOTES

try boast incredible natural views and a wide variety of outdoor activities. However, with these offerings the National Park System has a fairly firm on and off season due to inclement weather throughout much of the United States. As of 2016, the most popular national park was Great Smoky Mountains National Park in Tennessee and North Carolina, followed by Grand Canyon National Park and Yosemite. Jeff Olson, a spokesman for the NPS, speculates that Great Smoky's popularity stems from a combination of its free admission and proximity to Interstate 40, making it easily accessible for people in many southern cities, such as Atlanta, Nashville, and Louisville (Flowers). All three of the most popular national parks advertise hundreds of acres of land and miles of trails to be explored. However, as with many of the current national parks, the number of visitors is greatly affected by the weather. Pam Ziesler, a program coordinator for the NPS' Visitor Use Statistics, states that one theory behind the rise in national park popularity in 2015 and 2016 has to do with the temperate weather during "shoulder seasons," such as fall and spring, when bad weather can keep people out of the outdoor areas (Flowers). The NPS Visitor Use Statistics indicate that the majority of the parks experience peak visitation from May to September, when the weather is warm and most students are out of school (Welcome to Visitor Use Statistics). By increasing the number of parks designed around non-outdoor related activities, the NPS could exponentially increase visitorship during the traditional seasonal off-season.

By improving the year-round popularity of parks, more than just the park service will benefit. The building of new parks means an immediate bump to the local economies of towns surrounding the park area. According to Headwater Economics, areas that surround the parks end up with benefits that extend beyond tourism, and the opportunities created by protected lands and national park resources "attract and retain people, entrepreneurs, businesses, and retirees." The thousands of visitors to the area not only add millions of dollars to national economies throughout the country, but they also create thousands of jobs (Economic Impact of Parks). If new parks were created to celebrate more than just natural elements, areas struggling with poor economies that may not be surrounded by nature could possibly build new parks that will help to support the people in their town. This could mean major assistance for dying neighborhoods and towns that were once popular but no longer have strong businesses. As with any major change, there are individuals opposed to expanding the National Park Service throughout the country. Many of these people argue that there are already more National Parks than can be supported by tourism, and that the maintenance and repair costs allocated by the national budget are drawing valuable money away from other potential uses. Others argue that the National Park Service often oversteps their bounds by placing claims of protection on land that could be used to support companies that need natural resources, like mining and logging. However, not only do National Parks stimulate the economies of towns across the country, as explained earlier, they also provide and protect numerous resources that are priceless.

It is the mission of the National Parks to protect the animals, landscapes, and historical cultures of America. With thousands of plant and animal species facing extinction as their habitats are destroyed, the National Park Service provide "safe space for wildlife to breed and survive" ("5 Reasons Why"). Similarly, with so many Native American tribes living apart, the National Parks are their main way of protecting their culture and history for future generations. Plus, National Parks provide the public with thousands of acres of space for healthy exercise and recreation. Currently, West Virginia has the highest adult obesity rate in the United States with 37.7%, and is ranked as one of the most physically inactive states in the country ("Obesity Rates & Trends"). With an increase in National Parks, and a wider variety of topics to inter-

Vogelpohl   5

est potential visitors, more people would head to the parks for some, much needed, physical exercise.

Ultimately, it is clear that National Parks contribute greatly to American society, providing more than just tourism money but also physical benefits and protection for history, culture, and wildlife. My own family spent many vacations at National Parks, and I believe that is where my interest in both history and the environment comes from. It is something that I hope will be available to share with my own family later in life. However, I also understand that the creation of more National Parks would cost a significant amount of money. But how much is too high a price to pay for preserving nature and history for future generations? The benefits of the National Park Services should be expanded on, immediately, rather than ignored in favor of industrialism. The parks should take advantage of their recent rise in popularity to shed some needed light on those historical figures and accomplishments that are most often ignored. Not only will these new parks help the park system itself, with a hopeful increase in visitors who would not normally go to the parks, but increasing the number of parks will also improve the areas in which the parks are built by stimulating their economies. It is up to the American people to contact their local government officials and request the building of new and more diverse National Parks.

Works Cited

"5 Reasons Why National Parks and Wildlife Sanctuaries are So Important." *Visitor Guard*, 2015, https://www.visitorguard.com/ five-reasons-why-national-parks-and-wildlife-sanctuaries-are-so-important/.

"Centennial Incrventives." *National Park Service*, https://www.nps.gov/subjects/ centennial/nps-centennial-programs.htm.

NOTES

"Economic Impact of National Parks." *Headwaters Economics*, April 2017,
https://headwaterseconomics.org/public-lands/protected-lands/
economic-impact-of-national-parks/.

Errick, Jennifer. "Trivia Challenge: The 8 National Parks Devoted to Women's History."
National Parks Conservation Association, 1 March 2016, https://www.npca.
org/articles/1142-trivia-challenge-the-8-national-parks-devoted-to-
women-s-history.

Flowers, Andrew. "The National Parks Have Never Been More Popular."
FiveThirtyEight, 25 May 2016, https://fivethirtyeight.com/features/
the-national-parks-have-never-been-more-popular/.

"Obesity Rates & Trends." *The State of Obesity*, Aug 2017, https://stateofobesity.org/
rates/.

Root, Tiki. "Changing the Face of National Parks." *National Geographic*,
1 Feb 2017, https://news.nationalgeographic.com/2017/02/
diversity-in-national-parks/.

Thakar, Nidhi and Mark Magana. "Celebrating Hispanic Heritage Through Our
National Parks." *Huffpost*, 29 Sept 2015, https://www.huffingtonpost.com/
nidhi-thakar/celebrating-hispanic-heritage-national-parks_b_8215370.
html?1443546901.

"Welcome to Visitor Use Statistics." *NPS Stats*, 2017, https://irma.nps.gov/Stats/.

Telling Your English 101 Story

In this chapter, you will write in order to tell your story about your time in English 101 and how it has shaped you as a writer. You will revise and polish your work from the semester in order to be graded on your best work that demonstrates everything you know.

GETTING STARTED

One of the best ways to get started on your final portfolio for English 101 is to complete a Writer's Inventory. That means gathering all of your projects, writing exercises, feedback, and other documents to sit down and plan your next steps. (There is also an excellent description of this activity in *Easy Writer*.) Once you have everything together read it and start making a list of all of the things you want to do and show in your final portfolio.

PURPOSE

Like the midterm portfolio, the primary purpose of this assignment is to reflect on and document how you've improved as a writer throughout the course. Also like the midterm portfolio, it's often helpful to imagine that your portfolio makes an argument to your audience about how you've improved as a writer. In other words, the thesis of your midterm portfolio might be something like this:

> "Now that the course has ended I am confident I have improved <u>a little / somewhat / a lot</u> as a writer."

Your reflection, your projects, and your other writing are the evidence to support the claim you're making about your writing.

Remember: At this point, your final portfolio is worth 70% of your overall course grade.

AUDIENCE

Your primary audience for this project is your instructor for the course. With that understood, there may be some other audiences worth imagining. For example, some students have had success imagining an audience unfamiliar with their work like another English 101 instructor, a Dean at WVU, or a potential employer.

How does imagining a different audience affect your strategy for completing your portfolio?

CONVENTIONS

Typical final portfolios contain a reflective element (for example, a memo, cover letter, or preface) along with polished, revised copies of all four major projects in the course. Here are a few other characteristics of conventional portfolios:

- Reflective element is two to three pages long (600–900 words).

- Overall the portfolio is twenty or more pages long (about 6,000–7,000 words).

- Successful students arrange their portfolios in many different ways. Some include projects in their original order. Others arrange the projects from their worst to their best. Still others arrange them from their least improved to their most improved. The most important thing is to explain your choice.

TROUBLE SPOTS

Here are a few trouble spots regarding final portfolios. Think about what decisions you will make in order to address these questions:

- How are you backing up your work on a computer? You don't want to lose the whole thing the night before it's due!

- How will you shape the way your audience encounters your work? Will you highlight your changes? Annotate them? Include a reflective preface before each project?

ASSESSMENT

As at the midterm, all English 101 courses have the same core criteria for evaluating portfolios. There are two places in this book that you can look at for portfolio assessment criteria. The first is on the back inside cover of this book. This is really more of a checklist to help you think about and reflect on the course goals. The second place is the rubric on pages x–xiii that describes what superior portfolios look like, what strong portfolios look like, what satisfactory portfolios look like, and so on.

FREEWRITE

Remember freewriting is an activity meant to help you come up with ideas and record them. Recall too that there are two rules for freewriting aimed at helping you get the most out of the activity:

1. **Do not worry about spelling, grammar, and punctuation.**

2. **Do not stop writing.**

In order to start shaping your portfolio, take 3 minutes right now to do a freewrite on rhetoric. In other words, write down everything you know about rhetoric—all the ideas, terms, applications, strategies, questions, you name it—as quickly as you can. Ready. Set. Go!

_____

_____

_____

_____

_____

_____

_____

_____

_____

_____

_____

_____

_____

_____

_____

_____

_____

_____

_____

_____

_____

_____

_____

Great work! You've already started shaping the reflective introduction to your portfolio. Much of what you've written here can be valuable information for that document. Try repeating this activity for the other course goals.

MAKING A REVISION PLAN

At the end of the semester students often have a lot of work to do and not much time to do it. Therefore, it helps to be thoughtful about how you're spending your time. Instead of working your way through all of your projects in the order you did them, use this form to help you identify where you need to spend the most time and what you can accomplish most quickly.

Project #1: Narrative

My final-for-now draft was at the brainstorming/discussion/professional stage.

I've spent _____ hours on this project since I turned in my final-for-now draft.

If I had two more days to work on this project, I would need to . . .

_____

_____

_____

_____

_____

Project #2: Profile

My final-for-now draft was at the brainstorming/discussion/professional stage.

I've spent _____ hours on this project since I turned in my final-for-now draft.

If I had two more days to work on this project, I would need to . . .

_____

_____

_____

_____

_____

Project #3: Analysis

My final-for-now draft was at the brainstorming/discussion/professional stage.

I've spent _____ hours on this project since I turned in my final-for-now draft.

If I had two more days to work on this project, I would need to . . .

_____

_____

_____

_____

_____

Project #4: Exploratory Essay

My final-for-now draft was at the brainstorming/discussion/professional stage.

I've spent _____ hours on this project since I turned in my final-for-now draft.

If I had two more days to work on this project, I would need to . . .

_____

_____

_____

_____

_____

Now that you've thought about each project you need to choose a strategy for revision that works for you. Will you start with the one that needs the most work so that you can be certain you have time to make significant improvements? Will you start with the one that needs the least amount of work so that you can finish it quickly and focus on other ones? You'll need to decide for yourself based on your available time, work load, and energy level.

And remember, sometimes it can help to discuss your plan with someone. Try reviewing your plan with your instructor, a friend, or a consultant in the Eberly Writing Studio.

ADDITIONAL READING

Bird by Bird: Some Instructions on Writing and Life

ANNE LAMOTT

The first useful concept is the idea of short assignments. Often when you sit down to write, what you have in mind is an autobiographical novel about your childhood, or a play about the immigrant experience, or a history of—oh, say—women. But this is like trying to scale a glacier. It's hard to get your footing, and your fingertips get all red and frozen and torn up. Then your mental illnesses arrive at the desk like your sickest, most secretive relatives. And they pull up chairs in a semicircle around the computer, and they try to be quiet but you know they are there with their weird coppery breath, leering at you behind your back.

What I do at this point, as the panic mounts and the jungle drums begin beating and I realize that the well has run dry and that my future is behind me and I'm going to have to get a job only I'm completely unemployable, is to stop. First I try to breathe, because I'm either sitting there panting like a lapdog or I'm unintentionally making slow asthmatic death rattles. So I just sit there for a minute, breathing slowly, quietly. I let my mind wander. After a moment I may notice that I'm trying to decide whether or not I am too old for orthodontia and whether right now would be a good time to make a few calls, and then I start to think about learning to use makeup and how maybe I could find some boyfriend who is not a total and complete fixer-upper and then my life would be totally great and I'd be happy all the time, and then I think about all the people I should have called back before I sat down to work, and how

---

I should probably at least check in with my agent and tell him this great idea I have and see if *he* thinks it's a good idea, and see if he thinks I need orthodontia—if that is what he is actually thinking whenever we have lunch together. Then I think about someone I'm really annoyed with, or some financial problem that is driving me crazy, and decide that I must resolve this before I get down to today's work. So I become a dog with a chew toy, worrying it for a while, wrestling it to the ground, flinging it over my shoulder, chasing it, licking it, chewing it, flinging it back over my shoulder. I stop just short of actually barking. But all of this only takes somewhere between one and two minutes, so I haven't actually wasted that much time. Still, it leaves me winded. I go back to trying to breathe, slowly and calmly, and I finally notice the one-inch picture frame that I put on my desk to remind me of short assignments.

It reminds me that all I have to do is to write down as much as I can see through a one-inch picture frame. This is all I have to bite off for the time being. All I am going to do right now, for example, is write that one paragraph that sets the story in my hometown, in the late fifties, when the trains were still running. I am going to paint a picture of it, in words, on my word processor. Or all I am going to do is to describe the main character the very first time we meet her, when she first walks out the front door and onto the porch. I am not even going to describe the expression on her face when she first notices the blind dog sitting behind the wheel of her car—just what I can see through the one-inch picture frame, just one paragraph describing this woman, in the town where I grew up, the first time we encounter her.

E. L. Doctorow once said that "writing a novel is like driving a car at night. You can see only as far as your headlights, but you can make the whole trip that way." You don't have to see where you're going, you don't have to see your destination or everything you will pass along the way. You just have to see two or three feet ahead of you. This is right up there with the best advice about writing, or life, I have ever heard.

So after I've completely exhausted myself thinking about the people I most resent in the world, and my more arresting financial problems, and, of course, the orthodontia, I remember to pick up the one-inch picture frame and to figure out a one-inch piece of my story to tell, one small scene, one memory, one exchange. I also remember a story that I know I've told elsewhere but that over and over helps me to get a grip: thirty years ago my older brother, who was ten years old at the time, was trying to get a report on birds written that he'd had three months to write, which was due the next day. We were out at our family cabin in Bolinas, and he was at the kitchen table close to tears, surrounded by binder paper and pencils and unopened books on birds, immobilized by the hugeness of the task ahead. Then my father sat down beside him, put his arm around my brother's shoulder, and said, "Bird by bird, buddy. Just take it bird by bird."

I tell this story again because it usually makes a dent in the tremendous sense of being overwhelmed that my students experience. Sometimes it actually gives them hope, and hope, as Chesterton said, is the power of being cheerful in circumstances that we know to be desperate. Writing can be a pretty desperate endeavor, because it is about some of our deepest needs: our need to be visible, to be heard, our need to make sense of our lives, to wake up and grow and belong. It is no wonder if we sometimes tend to take ourselves perhaps a bit too seriously. So here is another story I tell often.

In the Bill Murray movie *Stripes*, in which he joins the army, there is a scene that takes place the first night of boot camp, where Murray's platoon is assembled in the barracks. They are supposed to be getting to know their sergeant, played by Warren Oates, and one another. So each man takes a few moments to say a few things about who he is and where he is from. Finally it is the turn of this incredibly intense guy named Francis. "My name is Francis," he says. "No one calls me Francis—

anyone here calls me Francis and I'll kill them. And another thing. I don't like to be touched. Anyone here ever tries to touch me, I'll kill them," at which point Warren Oates jumps in and says, "Hey—lighten up, Francis."

This is not a bad line to have taped to the wall of your office. Say to yourself in the kindest possible way, Look, honey, all we're going to do for now is to write a description of the river at sunrise, or the young child swimming in the pool at the club, or the first time the man sees the woman he will marry. That is all we are going to do for now. We are just going to take this bird by bird. But we are going to finish this one short assignment.

SHITTY FIRST DRAFTS

Now, practically even better news than that of short assignments is the idea of shitty first drafts. All good writers write them. This is how they end up with good second drafts and terrific third drafts. People tend to look at successful writers, writers who are getting their books published and maybe even doing well financially, and think that they sit down at their desks every morning feeling like a million dollars, feeling great about who they are and how much talent they have and what a great story they have to tell; that they take in a few deep breaths, push back their sleeves, roll their necks a few times to get all the cricks out, and dive in, typing fully formed passages as fast as a court reporter. But this is just the fantasy of the uninitiated. I know some very great writers, writers you love, who write beautifully and have made a great deal of money, and not *one* of them sits down routinely feeling wildly enthusiastic and confident. Not one of them writes elegant first drafts. All right, one of them does, but we do not like her very much. We do not think that she has a rich inner life or that God likes her or can even stand her. (Although when I mentioned this to my priest friend Tom, he said you can safely assume you've created God in your own image when it turns out that God hates all the same people you do.)

Very few writers really know what they are doing until they've done it. Nor do they go about their business feeling dewy and thrilled. They do not type a few stiff warm-up sentences and then find themselves bounding along like huskies across the snow. One writer I know tells me that he sits down every morning and says to himself nicely, "It's not like you don't have a choice, because you do—you can either type or kill yourself." We all often feel like we are pulling teeth, even those writers whose prose ends up being the most natural and fluid. The right words and sentences just do not come pouring out like ticker tape most of the time. Now, Muriel Spark is said to have felt that she was taking dictation from God every morning—sitting there, one supposes, plugged into a Dictaphone typing away, humming. But this is a very hostile and aggressive position. One might hope for bad things to rain down on a person like this.

For me and most of the other writers I know, writing is not rapturous. In fact, the only way I can get anything written at all is to write really, really shitty first drafts.

The first draft is the child's draft, where you let it all pour out and then let it romp all over the place, knowing that no one is going to see it and that you can shape it later. You just let this childlike part of you channel whatever voices and visions come through and onto the page. If one of the characters wants to say, "Well, so what, Mr. Poopy Pants?," you let her. No one is going to see it. If the kid wants to get into really sentimental, weepy, emotional territory, you let him. Just get it all down on paper, because there may be something great in those six crazy pages that you would never have gotten to by more rational, grown-up means. There may be something in the very last line of the very last paragraph on page six that you just love, that is so beautiful or wild that you now know what you're supposed to be writing about, more or less, or in what direction you might go—but there was no way to get to this without first getting through the first five and a half pages.

I used to write food reviews for *California* magazine before it folded. (My writing food reviews had nothing to do with the magazine folding, although every single review did cause a couple of canceled subscriptions. Some readers took umbrage at my comparing mounds of vegetable puree with various ex-presidents' brains.) These reviews always took two days to write. First I'd go to a restaurant several times with a few opinionated articulate friends in tow. I'd sit there writing down everything anyone said that was at all interesting or funny. Then on the following Monday I'd sit down at my desk with my notes, and try to write the review. Even after I'd been doing this for years, panic would set in. I'd try to write a lead, but instead I'd write a couple of dreadful sentences, XX them out, try again, XX everything out, and then feel despair and worry settle on my chest like an x-ray apron. It's over, I'd think, calmly. I'm not going to be able to get the magic to work this time. I'm ruined. I'm through. I'm toast. Maybe, I'd think, I can get my old job back as a clerk-typist. But probably not. I'd get up and study my teeth in the mirror for a while. Then I'd stop, remember to breathe, make a few phone calls, hit the kitchen and chow down. Eventually I'd go back and sit down at my desk, and sigh for the next ten minutes. Finally I would pick up my one-inch picture frame, stare into it as if for the answer, and every time the answer would come: all I had to do was to write a really shitty first draft of, say, the opening paragraph. And no one was going to see it.

So I'd start writing without reining myself in. It was almost just typing, just making my fingers move. And the writing would be *terrible*. I'd write a lead paragraph that was a whole page, even though the entire review could only be three pages long, and then I'd start writing up descriptions of the food, one dish at a time, bird by bird, and the critics would be sitting on my shoulders, commenting like cartoon characters. They'd be pretending to snore, or rolling their eyes at my over-wrought descriptions, no matter how hard I tried to tone those descriptions down, no matter how conscious I was of what a friend said to me gently in my early days of restaurant reviewing. "Annie," she said, "it is just a piece of *chicken*. It is just a bit of *cake*."

But because by then I had been writing for so long, I would eventually let myself trust the process—sort of, more or less. I'd write a first draft that was maybe twice as long as it should be, with a self-indulgent and boring beginning, stupefying descriptions of the meal, lots of quotes from my black-humored friends that made them sound more like the Manson girls than food lovers, and no ending to speak of. The whole thing would be so long and incoherent and hideous that for the rest of the day I'd obsess about getting creamed by a car before I could write a decent second draft. I'd worry that people would read what I'd written and believe that the accident had really been a suicide, that I had panicked because my talent was waning and my mind was shot.

The next day, though, I'd sit down, go through it all with a colored pen, take out everything I possibly could, find a new lead somewhere on the second page, figure out a kicky place to end it, and then write a second draft. It always turned out fine, sometimes even funny and weird and helpful. I'd go over it one more time and mail it in.

Then, a month later, when it was time for another review, the whole process would start again, complete with the fears that people would find my first draft before I could rewrite it.

Almost all good writing begins with terrible first efforts. You need to start somewhere. Start by getting something—anything—down on paper. A friend of mine says that the first draft is the down draft—you just get it down. The second draft is the up draft—you fix it up. You try to say what you have to say more accurately. And the third draft is the dental draft, where you check every tooth, to see if it's loose or cramped or decayed, or even, God help us, healthy.

What I've learned to do when I sit down to work on a shitty first draft is to quiet the voices in my head. First there's the vinegar-lipped Reader Lady, who says primly, "Well, *that's* not very interesting, is it?" And there's the emaciated German male who writes these Orwellian memos detailing your thought crimes. And there are your parents, agonizing over your lack of loyalty and discretion; and there's William Burroughs, dozing off or shooting up because he finds you as bold and articulate as a houseplant; and so on. And there are also the dogs: let's not forget the dogs, the dogs in their pen who will surely hurtle and snarl their way out if you ever stop writing, because writing is, for some of us, the latch that keeps the door of the pen closed, keeps those crazy ravenous dogs contained.

Quieting these voices is at least half the battle I fight daily. But this is better than it used to be. It used to be 87 percent. Left to its own devices, my mind spends much of its time having conversations with people who aren't there. I walk along defending myself to people, or exchanging repartee with them, or rationalizing my behavior, or seducing them with gossip, or pretending I'm on their TV talk show or whatever.

I speed or run an aging yellow light or don't come to a full stop, and one nanosecond later am explaining to imaginary cops exactly why I had to do what I did, or insisting that I did not in fact do it.

I happened to mention this to a hypnotist I saw many years ago, and he looked at me very nicely. At first I thought he was feeling around on the floor for the silent alarm button, but then he gave me the following exercise, which I still use to this day.

Close your eyes and get quiet for a minute, until the chatter starts up. Then isolate one of the voices and imagine the person speaking as a mouse. Pick it up by the tail and drop it into a mason jar. Then isolate another voice, pick it up by the tail, drop it in the jar. And so on. Drop in any high-maintenance parental units, drop in any contractors, lawyers, colleagues, children, anyone who is whining in your head. Then put the lid on, and watch all these mouse people clawing at the glass, jabbering away, trying to make you feel like shit because you won't do what they want—won't give them more money, won't be more successful, won't see them more often. Then imagine that there is a volume-control button on the bottle. Turn it all the way up for a minute, and listen to the stream of angry, neglected, guilt-mongering voices. Then turn it all the way down and watch the frantic mice lunge at the glass, trying to get to you. Leave it down, and get back to your shitty first draft.

A writer friend of mine suggests opening the jar and shooting them all in the head. But I think he's a little angry, and I'm sure nothing like this would ever occur to you.

SOMEONE TO READ YOUR DRAFTS

There's an old *New Yorker* cartoon of two men sitting on a couch at a busy cocktail party, having a quiet talk. One man has a beard and looks like a writer. The other seems like a normal person. The writer type is saying to the other, "We're still pretty far apart. I'm looking for a six-figure advance, and they're refusing to read the manuscript."

Now, I've been wrong before, but I'd bet you anything that this guy never shows his work to other writers before trying to get someone to buy it. I bet he thinks he's above that.

Whenever I'm giving a lecture at a writing conference and happen to mention the benefits of finding someone to read your drafts, at least one older established writer comes up to me and says that he or she would never in a million years show his or her work to another person before it was done. It is not a good idea, and I must stop telling my students that it will help them. I just smile, geishalike, and make little fluttery sounds of understanding. Then I go on telling people to consider finding someone who would not mind reading their drafts and marking them up with useful suggestions. The person may not have an answer to what is missing or annoying about the piece, but writing is so often about making mistakes and feeling lost. There are probably a number of ways to tell your story right, and someone else may be able to tell you whether or not you've found one of these ways.

I'm not suggesting that you and another writer sit in a cubby somewhere and write together, as though you were doing potato prints side by side at the institution, and that then you beam at each other's work the way you gape when your kid first writes his name. But I am suggesting that there may be someone out there in the world—maybe a spouse, maybe a close friend—who will read your finished drafts and give you an honest critique, let you know what does and doesn't work, give you some suggestions on things you might take out or things on which you need to collaborate, ways in which to make your piece stronger.

In the first story of Donald Barthelme's I ever read, twenty years ago, he said that truth is a hard apple to catch and it is a hard apple to throw. I know what a painful feeling it is when you've been working on something forever and it feels done, and you give your story to someone you hope will validate this and that person tells you it still needs more work. You have to, at this point, question your assessment of this person's character and, if he or she is not a spouse or a lifelong friend, decide whether or not you want them in your life at all. Mostly I think an appropriate first reaction is to think that you don't. But in a little while it may strike you as a small miracle that you have someone in your life, whose taste you admire (after all, this person loves you and your work), who will tell you the truth and help you stay on the straight and narrow or find your way back to it if you are lost.

I always show my work to one or two people before sending a copy to my editor or agent. I feel more secure and connected this way, and these two people get a lot of good work out of me. They are like midwives; there are these stories and ideas and visions and memories and plots inside me, and only I can give birth to them. Theoretically I could do it alone, but it makes it easier to have people helping. I have girlfriends who've had their babies through natural childbirth—no drugs, no spinal, no nothing—and they secretly think they had a more honest birth experience, but I think the epidural is right up there with the most important breakthroughs in the West, like the Salk polio vaccine and salad bars in supermarkets. It's an individual thing. What works for me may not work for you. But feedback from someone I'm close to gives me confidence, or at least it gives me time to improve. Imagine that you are getting ready for a party and there is a person at your house who can check you out and assure you that you look wonderful or, conversely, that you actually do look a little tiny tiny tiny bit heavier than usual in this one particular dress or suit or that red makes you look just a bit like you have sarcoptic mange. Of course you are disappointed for a moment, but then you are grateful that you are still in the privacy of your own home and there is time to change.

One of the best writers I know has a wife who reads everything he writes and tells him when she loves it and when she doesn't, why it does or doesn't work for her. She is almost like an equal partner in the process. Two other writers I know use each other. As I said, I have two people who read my stuff. One is another writer, who is one of my best friends and probably the most neurotic, mentally ill person in my galaxy. Another is a librarian who reads two or three books a week but has never written a word. What I do is to work over a piece until it feels just about right, and then I send it to one of these two friends, who have agreed in advance to read it.

I always send my work Federal Express, because I am too impatient to wait for the mail to deliver it. I spend the entire next day waiting to hear, pacing, overeating, feeling paranoid and badly treated if I haven't heard from my friends by noon. Naturally I assume that they think it is tripe but that they don't have the courage to tell me. Then I'll think about all the things I don't like about either of them, how much in fact I hate them both, how it is no wonder that neither of them has many friends. And then the phone will ring and they usually say something along the lines of "I think it's going to be great, I think it's really good work. But I also think there are a few problems."

At this point, I am usually open to suggestion, because I am so relieved that they think it's going to be great. And I ask gaily where they think there's room for improvement. This is where things can get ever so slightly dicey. They might say that the whole first half is slow, and they couldn't get into it, but that on page six or thirty-eight or whatever, things finally got going, and then they couldn't put it down. They absolutely raced through the rest of it—except that maybe they had a bit of trouble with the ending, and they wonder if I really understand one character's motivation and whether I might just want to spend—oh—five minutes, no more, rethinking this person.

My first response if they have a lot of suggestions is never profound relief that I have someone in my life who will be honest with me and help me do the very best work of which I am capable. No, my first thought is, "Well. I'm sorry, but I can't be friends with you anymore, because you have too many problems. And you have a bad personality. And a bad character."

Sometimes I can't get words to come out of my mouth because I am so disappointed as if they had said that Sam is ugly and boring and spoiled and I should let him go. Criticism is very hard to take. But then whichever friend is savaging my work will suggest that we go through it together page by page, line by line, and in a clipped, high-pitched voice I'll often suggest that this won't be necessary, that everything's just fine. But these friends usually talk me into going through the manuscript with them over the phone, and if I'll hang in there, they'll have found a number of places where things could be so much stronger, or funnier, or more real, or more interesting, or less tedious. They may even have ideas on how to fix those places, and so, by the end, I am breathing a great sigh of relief and even gratitude.

When someone reliable gives you this kind of feedback, you now have some true sense of your work's effect on people, and you may now know how to approach your final draft. If you are getting ready to send your work to a potential agent for the first time, you don't want to risk burning that bridge by sending something that's just not ready.

You really must get your piece or book just right, as right as you can. Sometimes it is just a matter of fine-tuning, or maybe one whole character needs to be rethought. Sometimes the friend will love the feel of the writing, the raw material, and yet feel that it is a million miles from being done. This can be deeply disappointing, but again, better that your spouse or friend tell you this than an agent or an editor.

I heard Marianne Williamson say once, that when you ask God into your life, you think he or she is going to come into your psychic house, look around, and see that you just need a new floor or better furniture and that everything needs just a little cleaning—and so you go along for the first six months thinking how nice life is now that God is there. Then you look out the window one day and see there's a wrecking ball outside. It turns out that God actually thinks your whole foundation is shot and that you're going to have to start over from scratch. This is exactly what it can be like to give, say, a novel to someone else to read. This person can love it and still find it a total mess, in need of a great deal of work, of even a new foundation.

So how do I find one of these partners? my students ask. The same way you find a number of people for a writing group. The only difference is that in this case, you're looking for one partner instead of several. So if you are in a class, look around, see if there's someone whose work you've admired, who seems to be at about the same level as you. Then you can ask him or her if he or she wants to meet for a cup of coffee and see if you can work with each other. It's like asking for a date, so while you are doing this, you will probably be rolfed by all your most heinous memories of seventh and eighth grade. If the person says no, it's good to wait until you get inside your car before you fall apart completely. Then you can rend your clothes and keen and do a primal scream. Of course, you probably want to be sure that the person hasn't followed you out to your car. But it actually doesn't matter if he or she sees you break down, because you don't have to be friendly with that person anymore. That person is a jerk. You double up therapy sessions for a few weeks until you're back in the saddle, and then you ask someone else; someone you like much better.

If you know for sure that some smart and civilized person loves your work, you can ask that person if she would be willing to look at a part of your novel or your latest short story. If this person writes, too, ask if she would like you to take a look at her draft. If she says no to both offers, pretend to be friendly, so she won't think less of you than she already does. Then you can move into a trailer park near your therapist's home until you're well enough again to ask someone else.

The second question my students ask about a writing partner is this: what if someone agrees to read and work on your stuff for you, and you have agreed to do the same for him, say, and it turns out that he says things about your work, even in the nicest possible tone of voice, that are totally negative and destructive? You find your-self devastated, betrayed. Here you've done this incredibly gutsy thing, shown some-one your very heart and soul, and he doesn't think it's any good. He says how sorry he is that this is how he feels. Well, let me tell you this—I don't think he is. I think de-stroying your work gave him real pleasure, pleasure he would never cop to, pleasure that is almost sexual in nature. I think you should get rid of this person immediately, even if you are married to him. No one should talk to you like this. If you write a long piece, and it is your first, and you are wondering if it's publishable, and it isn't, even by a long shot, someone should be able to tell you this in a way that is gentle yet not patronizing, so that you are encouraged—maybe not to pursue publication, but to pursue writing. Certainly this person might suggest you get a second opinion. But if he is too strident or adamant, ditch the sucker. Would you stand for someone talking this way to your children—for instance, telling them that they are not very talented at painting and shouldn't even bother? Or that their poetry is not very interesting? Of course not. You'd want to go pay this person a little visit with your flame thrower. So why, if someone says something like this to you, would you want anything further to do with him? Why waste what little time you may have left with such scum?

I worry that Jesus drinks himself to sleep when he hears me talk like this. But about a month before my friend Pammy died, she said something that may have permanently changed me.

We had gone shopping for a dress for me to wear that night to a nightclub with the man I was seeing at the time. Pammy was in a wheelchair, wearing her Queen Mum wig, the *Easy Rider* look in her eyes. I tried on a lavender minidress, which is not my usual style. I tend to wear big, baggy clothes. People used to tell me I dressed like John Goodman. Anyway, the dress fit perfectly, and I came out to model it for her. I stood there feeling very shy and self-conscious and pleased. Then I said,

"Do you think it makes my hips look too big?" and she said to me slowly, "Annie? I really don't think you have that kind of time."

And I don't think you have that kind of time either. I don't think you have time to waste not writing because you are afraid you won't be good enough at it, and I don't think you have time to waste on someone who does not respond to you with kindness and respect. You don't want to spend your time around people who make you hold your breath. You can't fill up when you're holding your breath. And writing is about filling up, filling up when you are empty, letting images and ideas and smells run down like water—just as writing is also about dealing with the emptiness. The emptiness destroys enough writers without the help of some friend or spouse.

There are always a couple of rank beginners in my classes, and they need people to read their drafts who will rise to the occasion with respect and encouragement. Beginners always try to fit their whole lives into ten pages, and they always write blatantly about themselves, even if they make the heroine of their piece a championship racehorse with an alcoholic mother who cries a lot. But beginners are learning to play, and they need encouragement to keep their hands moving across the page.

If you look around, I think you will find the person you need. Almost every writer I've ever known has been able to find someone who could be both a friend and a critic. You'll know when the person is right for you and when you are right for that person. It's not unlike finding a mate, where little by little you begin to feel that you've stepped into a shape that was waiting there all along.

NOTES

Responding—Really Responding—to Other Students' Writing

RICHARD STRAUB

Okay. You've got a student paper you have to read and make comments on for Thursday. It's not something you're looking forward to. But that's alright, you think. There isn't really all that much to it. Just keep it simple. Read it quickly and mark whatever you see. Say something about the introduction. Something about details and examples. Ideas you can say you like. Mark any typos and spelling errors. Make your comments brief. Abbreviate where possible: *awk, good intro, give ex, frag.* Try to imitate the teacher. Mark what he'd mark and sound like he'd sound. But be cool about it. Don't praise anything really, but no need to get harsh or cutthroat either. Get in and get out. You're okay, I'm okay. Everybody's happy. What's the problem?

This is, no doubt, a way of getting through the assignment. Satisfy the teacher and no surprises for the writer. It might just do the trick. But say you want to do a *good* job. Say you're willing to put in the time and effort—though time is tight and you know it's not going to be easy—and help the writer look back on the paper and revise it. And maybe in the process learn something more yourself about writing. What do you look for? How do you sound? How much do you take up? What exactly are you trying to accomplish? Here are some ideas.

HOW SHOULD YOU LOOK AT YOURSELF AS A RESPONDER?

Consider yourself a friendly reader. A test pilot. A roommate who's been asked to look over the paper and tell the writer what you think. Except you don't just take on the role of The Nice Roommate or The Ever-Faithful Friend and tell her what she

---

"Responding—Really Responding—to Other Students' Writing" by Richard Straub from *The Subject is Writing, 4th Edition: Essays by Teachers and Students* by Wendy Bishop and James Strickland, Editors. Copyright © 2006 by Boynton/Cook Publishers, Inc. Published by Heinemann, Portsmouth, NH. Reprinted by permission of the publisher.

wants to hear. *This all looks good. I wouldn't change a thing. There are a couple places that I think he might not like, but I can see what you're doing there. I'd go with it. Good stuff.* You're supportive. You give her the benefit of the doubt and look to see the good in her writing. But friends don't let friends think their writing is the best thing since *The Great Gatsby* and they don't lead them to think that all is fine and well when it's not. Look to help this friend, this roommate writer—okay, this person in your class—to get a better piece of writing. Point to problems and areas for improvement but do it in a constructive way. See what you can do to push her to do even more than she's done and stretch herself as a writer.

WHAT ARE YOUR GOALS?

First, don't set out to seek and destroy all errors and problems in the writing. You're not an editor. You're not a teacher. You're not a cruise missile. And don't rewrite any parts of the paper. You're not the writer; you're a reader. One of many. The paper is not yours; it's the writer's. She writes. You read. She is in charge of what she does to her writing. That doesn't mean you can't make suggestions. It doesn't mean you can't offer a few sample rewrites here and there, as models. But make it clear they're samples, models. Not rewrites. Not edits. Not corrections. Be reluctant at first even to say what you would do if the paper were yours. It's not yours. Again: Writers write, readers read and show what they're understanding and maybe make suggestions. What to do instead: Look at your task as a simple one. You're there to play back to the writer how you read the paper: what you got from it; what you found interesting; where you were confused; where you wanted more. With this done, you can go on to point out problems, ask questions, offer advice, and wonder out loud with the writer about her ideas. Look to help her improve the writing or encourage her to work on some things as a writer.

HOW DO YOU GET STARTED?

Before you up and start reading the paper, take a minute (alright, thirty seconds) to make a mental checklist about the circumstances of the writing, the context. You're not going to just read a text. You're going to read a text within a certain context, a set of circumstances that accompany the writing and that you bring to your reading. It's one kind of writing or another, designed for one audience and purpose or another. It's a rough draft or a final draft. The writer is trying to be serious or casual, straight or ironic. Ideally, you'll read the paper with an eye to the circumstances that it was written in and the situation it is looking to create. That means looking at the writing in terms of the assignment, the writer's particular interests and aims, the work you've been doing in class, and the stage of drafting.

- *The assignment:* What kind of writing does the assignment call (or allow) for? Is the paper supposed to be a personal essay? A report? An analysis? An argument? Consider how well the paper before you meets the demands of the kind of writing the writer is taking up.

- *The writer's interests and aims:* What does the writer want to accomplish? If she's writing a personal narrative, say, is she trying to simply recount a past experience? Is she trying to recount a past experience and at the same time amuse her readers? Is she trying to show a pleasant experience on the surface, yet suggest underneath that everything was not as pleasant as it seems? Hone in on the writer's particular aims in the writing.

- *The work of the class:* Try to tie your comments to the concepts and strategies you've been studying in class. If you've been doing a lot of work on using detail, be sure to point to places in the writing where the writer uses detail effectively or where she might provide richer detail. If you've been working on developing arguments through examples and sample cases, indicate where the writer might use such methods to strengthen her arguments. If you've been considering various ways to sharpen the style of your sentences, offer places where the writer can clarify her sentence structure or arrange a sentence for maximum impact. The best comments will ring familiar even as they lead the writer to try to do something she hasn't quite done before, or done in quite the same way. They'll be comforting and understandable even as they create some need to do more, a need to figure out some better way.

- *The stage of drafting:* Is it an early draft? A full but incomplete draft? A nearly final draft? Pay attention to the stage of drafting. Don't try to deal with everything all at once if it's a first, rough draft. Concentrate on the large picture: the paper's focus; the content; the writer's voice. Don't worry about errors and punctuation problems yet. There'll be time for them later. If it's closer to a full draft, go ahead and talk, in addition to the overall content, about arrangement, pacing, and sentence style. Wait till the final draft to give much attention to fine-tuning sentences and dealing in detail with proofreading. Remember: You're not an editor. Leave these sentence revisions and corrections for the writer. It's her paper. And she's going to learn best by detecting problems and making her own changes.

WHAT TO ADDRESS IN YOUR COMMENTS?

Try to focus your comments on a couple of areas of writing. Glance through the paper quickly first. Get an idea whether you'll deal mostly with the overall content and purpose of the writing, its shape and flow, or (if these are more or less in order) with local matters of paragraph structure, sentence style, and correctness. Don't try to cover everything that comes up or even all instances of a given problem. Address issues that are most important to address in this paper, at this time.

WHERE TO PUT YOUR COMMENTS?

Some teachers like to have students write comments in the margins right next to the passage. Some like to have students write out their comments in an end note or in a separate letter to the writer. I like to recommend using both marginal comments and a note or letter at the end. The best of both worlds. Marginal comments allow you to give a quick moment-by-moment reading of the paper. They make it easy to give immediate and specific feedback. You still have to make sure you specify what you're talking about and what you have to say, but they save you some work telling the writer what you're addressing and allow you to focus your end note on things that are most important. Comments at the end allow you to provide some perspective on your response. This doesn't mean that you have to size up the paper and give it a thumbs up or a thumbs down. You can use the end comment to emphasize the key points of your response, explain and elaborate on issues you want to deal with more fully, and mention additional points that you don't want to address in detail. One thing to avoid: plastering comments all over the writing; in between and over the lines of the other person's writing—up, down, and across the page. Write in your space, and let the writer keep hers.

HOW TO SOUND?

Not like a teacher. Not like a judge. Not like an editor or critic or shotgun. (Wouldn't you want someone who was giving you comments not to sound like a teacher's red pen, a judge's ruling, an editor's impatience, a critic's wrath, a shotgun's blast?) Sound like you normally sound when you're speaking with a friend or acquaintance. Talk to the writer. You're not just marking up a text; you're responding to the writer. You're a reader, a helper, a colleague. Try to sound like someone who's a reader, who's helpful, and who's collegial. Supportive. And remember: Even when you're tough and demanding you can still be supportive.

HOW MUCH TO COMMENT?

Don't be stingy. Write most of your comments out in full statements. Instead of writing two or three words, write seven or eight. Instead of making only one brief comment and moving on, say what you have to say and then go back over the statement and explain what you mean or why you said it or note other alternatives. Let the writer know again and again how you are understanding her paper, what you take her to be saying. And elaborate on your key comments. Explain your interpretations, problems, questions, and advice.

IS IT OKAY TO BE SHORT AND SWEET?

No. At least not most of the time. Get specific. Don't rely on general statements alone. How much have generic comments helped you as a writer? "Add detail." "Needs better structure." "Unclear." Try to let the writer know what exactly the problem is. Refer specifically to the writer's words and make them a part of your comments. "Add some detail on what it was like working at the beach." "I think we'll need to know more about your high school crowd before we can understand the way you've changed." "This sentence is not clear. Were you disappointed or were they disappointed?" This way the writer will see what you're talking about, and she'll have a better idea what to work on.

DO YOU PRAISE OR CRITICIZE OR WHAT?

Be always of two (or three) minds about your response to the paper. You like the paper, but it could use some more interesting detail. You found this statement interesting, but these ideas in the second paragraph are not so hot. It's an alright paper, but it could be outstanding if the writer said what was really bothering her. Always be ready to praise. But always look to point to places that are not working well or that are not yet working as well as they might. Always be ready to expect more from the writer.

HOW TO PRESENT YOUR COMMENTS?

Don't steer away from being critical. Feel free—in fact, feel obliged—to tell the writer what you like and don't like, what is and is not working, and where you think it can be made to work better. But use some other strategies, too. Try to engage the writer in considering her choices and thinking about possible ways to improve the paper. Make it a goal to write two or three comments that look to summarize or paraphrase what the writer is saying. Instead of *telling* the reader what to do, *suggest* what she might do. Identify the questions that are raised for you as you reader:

- Play back your way of understanding the writing:

  This seems to be the real focus of the paper, the issue you seem most interested in.

  So you're saying that you really weren't interested in her romantically?

- Temper your criticisms:

  This sentence is a bit hard to follow.

  I'm not sure this paragraph is necessary.

- Offer advice:

  It might help to add an example here.

  Maybe save this sentence for the end of the paper.

- Ask questions, especially real questions:

  What else were you feeling at the time?

  What kind of friend? Would it help to say?

  Do you need this opening sentence?

  In what ways were you "a daddy's little girl"?

- Explain and follow up on your initial comments:

  You might present this episode first. This way we can see what you mean when you say that he was always too busy.

  How did you react? Did you cry or yell? Did you walk away?

  This makes her sound cold and calculating. Is that what you want?

- Offer some praise, and then explain to the writer why the writing works:

  > Good opening paragraph. You've got my attention.

  > Good detail. It tells me a lot about the place.

  > I like the descriptions you provide—for instance, about your grandmother cooking, at the bottom of page 1; about her house, in the middle of page 2; and about how she said her rosary at night: "quick but almost pleading, like crying without tears."

HOW MUCH CRITICISM? HOW MUCH PRAISE?

Challenge yourself to write as many praise comments as criticisms. When you praise, praise well. Think about it. Sincerity and specificity are everything when it comes to a compliment.

HOW MUCH SHOULD YOU BE INFLUENCED BY WHAT YOU KNOW ABOUT THE WRITER?

Consider the person behind the writer when you make your comments. If she's not done so well in class lately, maybe you can give her a pick-me-up in your comments. If she's shy and seems reluctant to go into the kind of personal detail the paper seems to need, encourage her. Make some suggestions or tell her what you would do. If she's confident and going on arrogant, see what you can do to challenge her with the ideas she presents in the paper. Look for other views she may not have thought about, and find ways to lead her to consider them. Always be ready to look at the text in terms of the writer behind the text.

Good comments, this listing shows, require a lot from a reader. But you don't have to make a checklist out of these suggestions and go through each one methodically as you read. It's amazing how they all start coming together when you look at your response as a way of talking with the writer seriously about the writing, recording how you experience the words on the page, and giving the writer something to think about for revision. The more you see examples of thoughtful commentary and the more you try to do it yourself, the more you'll get a feel for how it's done.

Here's a set of student comments on a student paper. They were done in the last third of a course that focused on the personal essay and concentrated on helping students develop the content and thought of their writing. The class had been working on finding ways to develop and extend the key statements of their essays (by using short, representative details, full-blown examples, dialogue, and multiple perspectives) and getting more careful about selecting and shaping parts of their writing. The assignment called on students to write an essay or an autobiographical story where they looked to capture how they see (or have seen) something about one or both of their parents—some habits, attitudes, or traits their parents have taken on. They were encouraged to give shape to their ideas and experiences in ways that went beyond their previous understandings and try things they hadn't tried in their writing. More a personal narrative than an essay, Todd's paper looks to capture one distinct difference in the way his mother and father disciplined their children. It is a rough draft that will be taken through one or possibly two more revisions. Readers were asked to offer whatever feedback they could that might help the writer with the next stage of writing (Figure 7-1).

Jeremy

Todd
ENG 1
Rick Straub
Assignment 8b

"Uh, oh"

When I called home from the police station I was praying that my father would answer the phone. He would listen to what I had to say and would react comely, logical, and in a manner that would keep my mother from screaming her head off. If my Mother was to answer the phone I would have to explain myself quickly in order to keep her from having a heart attack. *I like this paragraph. It immediately lets the reader relate to you and also places the reader right into the picture.*

When I was eleven years old I hung out with a group of boys that were almost three years older than me. The five of us did all the things that young energetic kids did playing ball, riding bikes, and getting in to trouble. [Because they were older they worried less about getting in trouble and the consequences of there actions than I did.] *Good point, makes it more unlikely that you should be the one to get caught?*

what other things did you do to get into trouble? is or is it irrelevant? My friends and I would always come home from school, drop our backpacks off and head out in the neighborhood to find something to do. Our favorite thing to do was to find construction cites and steal wood to make tree forts in the woods or skateboard ramps. So one day, coming home from school, we noticed a couple new houses being built near our neighborhood. It was a prime cite for wood, nails, and anything else we could get our hands on. We discussed our plan on the bus and decided that we would all meet there after dropping our stuff off at home. [I remember being a little at hesitant first because it was close to my house but beyond the boundaries my parents had set *of adventure* for me. *great passage really lets the reader know what you were thinking* Of course I went because I didn't want to be the odd man out and have to put up with all the name calling.] I dropped my bag off and I headed to the construction cite.

I meet my friends there and we began to search the different houses for wood and what not. We all picked up a couple of things and were about to leave when one of my friends noticed a what looked to be a big tool shed off behind one of the houses. It looked promising so we decided that we should check it out. Two of the boys in the group said that they had all the wood they could carry and said they were going home. The rest of us headed down to the shed to take a look.

Once there we noticed that the shed had been broken in to previously. The lock on it had been busted on the hinges were bent. *who tore* I opened the door to the shed and stepped inside to take a *a reason you* look around while my friends waited outside. It was dark inside *were first* but I could tell the place had been ransacked, there was nothing *or did it just* to take so I decided to leave. I heard my to friends say some *happen that* thing so turned back around to site of them running away. I *way* thought that they were playing a joke on me so I casually walked

Figure 7-1

133

out only to see a cop car parked near one of the houses under construction. As soon as I saw that cop car I took off but was stopped when a big hand pulled at that back of my shirt. I watched my friends run until they were out of cite and then I turned around.

The cop had me sit in the squad car while he asked me questions. He asked me if I knew those kids that ran off and I said "Nnnnnooooooooo". He asked me if I had broken in to that shed and I said "Nnnnnooooooo". The cop wrote down what I was saying all the while shaking his head. Then he told me that I wasn't being arrested but I would have to go down to the station to call parents and have them pick me up. Upon hearing that I nearly soiled my undershorts. "My God, I'm dead. My mom is going to kill me".

[handwritten margin note: what else happened at the police station? How long were you there?]

At the station the officer showed me the whole station, jail cells and everything. An obvious tactic to try and scare me, which worked. That plus the thought of my mom answering the phone and me trying to explain what happened nearly made me sick.

"Wwwwhhhaatttt! You're where?" She would say.

"The police station mom," uh oh, hear it comes.

"Ooooohhhh my God, my son is criminal," so loud I would have to pull the phone away from my ear.

[handwritten margin note: maybe you could say more so telling you think your mom is like this]

She had this uncanny ability to blow things out of proportion right from the start. She would assume the worse and then go from there. This was a classic example of why I could never go to her if I had any bad news. She would start screaming, get upset, and then go bitch at my father. My father is a pretty laid back but when ever my mother started yelling at him about me, he would get angry and come chew me out worse than if I had just gone to him in the first place.

If my father were to answer the phone he would respond with out raising his voice. He would examine the situation in a logical manner and make a decision form there.

"Uhhmmm(long pause). You're at the police station."

"Yeah dad, I didn't get arrested they just had me come down here so I had to tell you."

"Uhm, so you didn't get arrested(long pause). Well(long pause), I'll come pick you up and will talk about then".

[handwritten margin note: Did your Dad get into trouble as a kid so he knows what it's like? Explain why he reacts as he does.]

I feel like I can relate to my father much better then I can to my mother. He has a cool and collective voice that can take command of any situation. I always feel like he understands me, like he knows what I'm thinking all the time. This comes in real handy when I get in trouble.

[handwritten margin note: would he punish you anyway or could you just get away with things]

[handwritten margin note right side: I like the way you use dialogue in this section to illustrate how each of your parents would react and then explan to the reader what each of them are like. It works well.]

I called home. Sweet beading on my lip.

"Hello", my mom said. Oh geez, I'm dead.

"Mom can I talk to dad?"

"Why, what's wrong?"

"Oh, nothing, I just need talk to him," yes, this is going to work!

"Hold on," she said.

"Hello," my father said.

"Dad, I'm at the police station," I told him the whole story of what happened. He reacted exactly as I expect he would.

"Uhhmmm(long pause). You're at the police station.........

[handwritten note: I really like the ending, it tells the reader what is going to happen without having to explain it step by step. Good paper, I like the use of dialogue. Perhaps more on your understanding of why your parents react as they do.]

Figure 7-1 *continued*

This is a full and thoughtful set of comments. The responder, Jeremy, creates himself not as a teacher or critic but first of all as a reader, one who is intent on saying how he takes the writing and what he'd like to hear more about:

> Good point. Makes it more unlikely that you should be the one to get caught.
> Great passage. Really lets the reader know what you were thinking.
> Was there a reason you were first or did it just happen that way?
> Would he punish you anyway or could you just get away with things?

He makes twenty-two comments on the paper—seventeen statements in the margins and five more in the end note. The comments are written out in full statements, and they are detailed and specific. They make his response into a lively exchange with the writer, one person talking with another about what he's said. Well over half of the comments are follow-up comments that explain, illustrate, or qualify other responses.

The comments focus on the content and development of the writing, in line with the assignment, the stage of drafting, and the work of the course. They also view the writing rhetorically, in terms of how the text has certain effects on readers. Although there are over two dozen wording or sentence-level errors in the paper, he decides, wisely, to stick with the larger matters of writing. Yet even as he offers a pretty full set of comments he doesn't ever take control over the text. His comments are placed unobtrusively on the page, and he doesn't try to close things down or decide things for the writer. He offers praise, encouragement, and direction. What's more, he pushes the writer to do more than he has already done, to extend the boundaries of his examination. In keeping with the assignment and the larger goals of the course, he calls on Todd in several comments to explore the motivations and personalities behind his parents' different ways of disciplining:

> Maybe you could say more as to why you think your mom is like this.
> Did your dad get into trouble as a kid so he knows what it's like? Explain why he reacts as he does.

He is careful, though, not to get presumptuous and make decisions for the writer. Instead, he offers options and points to possibilities:

> Perhaps more on your understanding of why your parents react as they do. What other things did you do to get into trouble? Or is it irrelevant?

From start to finish he takes on the task of reading and responding and leaves the work of writing and revising to Todd.

Jeremy's response is not in a class by itself. A set of comments to end all commentary on Todd's paper. He might have done well, for instance, to recognize how much this paper works because of the way Todd arranges the story. He could have done more to point to what's not working in the writing or what could be made to work better. He might have asked Todd for more details about his state of mind when he got caught by the policeman and while he was being held at the police station. He might have urged him more to make certain changes. He might even have said, if only in a brief warning, something about the number of errors across the writing. But this is moot and just. Different readers are always going to pick up on different things and respond in different ways, and no one reading or response is going to address everything that might well be addressed, in the way it might best be addressed. All responses are incomplete and provisional—one reader's way of reading and reacting to the text in front of him. And any number of other responses, presented in any number of different ways, might be as useful or maybe even more useful to Todd as he takes up his work with the writing.

All this notwithstanding, Jeremy's comments are solid. They are full. They are thoughtful. And they are respectful. They take the writing and the writer seriously and address the issues that are raised responsibly. His comments do what commentary on student writing should optimally do. They turn the writer back into his writing and lead him to reflect on his choices and aims, to consider and reconsider his intentions as a writer and the effects the words on the page will have on readers. They help him see what he can work on in revision and what he might deal with in his ongoing work as a writer.

CHAPTER **7**

NOTES

JON SCOTT NELSON FIRST-YEAR WRITING AWARD

Sponsored by the WVU Department of English

Student Name _____

Local Address _____

_____

Phone Number (please provide number that is easiest to reach you at)

_____

Class Rank _____

Student ID # _____

Title(s) of Entry/ies   Genre(s)

_____   _____

_____   _____

_____   _____

_____   _____

Instructor's Name _____

Jon Scott Nelson Contest Guidelines

The Jon Scott Nelson Freshman Writing Award recognizes outstanding writing by English 101 students. All students enrolled in English 101 during the current academic year are eligible. Up to five prizes are awarded annually ($100 each). Please submit essays written in an English 101 class.

- Expository writing developed for your English 101 class only

- All submissions must have been written for classes *at WVU*.

- Students' names should be removed from the entries. Attach this entry form instead.

- No entries submitted after the March deadline (specific date to be announced in Spring) will be accepted.

For more information, e-mail Marsha.Bissett@mail.wvu.edu

WORKS CITED

"Annotate." *Merriam-Webster.com*. Merriam-Webster, 2015.

Carroll, Laura Bolin. "Backpacks Vs. Briefcases: Steps Toward Rhetorical Analysis." *WritingSpaces.org*, 2010, http://writingspaces.org/essays/backpacks-vs-briefcases, 3 Nov. 2014.

Bunn, Mike. "How to Read Like a Writer." *WritingSpaces.org*, 2011, http://writingspaces.org/bunn--how-to-read-like-a-writer 27 Mar. 2015.

Giles, Sandra. "Reflective Writing and the Revision Process: What Where You Thinking?" *WritingSpaces.org*, 2010, http://writingspaces.org/essays/reflective-writing-and-the-revision, 13 Mar. 2018.

Singh, Corcoran, Nathalie. "Composition as a Write of Passage." *WritingSpaces.org*, 2011, http://writingspaces.org/singh-corcoran--composition-as-a-write, 13 Mar. 2018.

Lunsford, Andrea A. *Easy Writer*. 6th ed. Bedford/St. Martin's, 2014.

Appendices

APPENDIX A: WRITING EXERCISES

These are writing exercises that the instructor may include as classroom activities or as homework.

Exercise—Diagnostic Writing (Option 1)

This is a simple writing activity aimed at helping me learn about you, your writing, and how you communicate.

To complete this activity write about one page (300 words) describing a time you communicated well.

Explain the purpose of the communication, who the audience was, and what the situation was. Also identify any trouble spots you encountered and how you overcame them.

Exercise—Diagnostic Writing (Option 2)

This is a simple writing activity aimed at helping me learn about you, your writing, and how you communicate.

To complete this activity write about one page (300 words) describing your writing process. What do you do when you have to write a paper for school? What steps do you follow? What about writing you do in other contexts, like at home or at work? Do you follow a similar process? In what ways, if any, is all of your writing connected?

GETTING A GRADE

This is a credit/no credit assignment. You will not receive a grade, but you will receive full credit if you complete the assignment according to the guidelines.

Exercise—Notes Page

Have you ever slogged through reading an entire book chapter and then, when you finally get to the last word, you ask yourself, "What did I just read?"

A notes page is a genre of document that helps its creator focus getting usable information out of a text. It has several benefits. First, instead of using cumbersome note cards, it provides you with an electronic format for recording quotes and other information you may want to refer to later. Second, it helps you read with a purpose so that you don't finish reading a chapter in a textbook and then wonder what it was about.

PARTS OF A NOTES PAGE

A notes page has several different parts, but they all help you focus on the reading.

- Citation—Start off the notes page with the citation for the document you're reading. That way, you can easily copy and paste it onto your Works Cited page when you are using it as a source for research.

- Summary—Next, write a short summary of the document. Focus on explaining the author's purpose and describing the evidence used. Do not use this space to only say if you liked the article.

- Notes—Use this section for things you want to remember about the article. For example, you might write down specific vocabulary words you want to remember or that are central to the author's argument. You may decide to combine this with the quotes section.

- Quotes—In this section, you write specific quotes that you think you might be able to use as evidence in a paper or that make the author's purpose clear.

- Queries—In this section, you will write questions about things you don't understand or that you want to do more research on. Always write one or two of these questions down if you will be discussing a reading in class.

- Connections—You use this last section to connect the document to other things you remember. That could be a note about a documentary film, a citation, or a quick blurb about how this thing you've read reminds me of something from your personal experience.

Creating notes pages is an excellent way to process the information you read regardless of whether or not you are reading for an English class. If you spend 10 minutes creating a notes page each time you have a reading assignment you will impress your peers and professors with your preparedness for class.

SAMPLE NOTES PAGE

MLA Citation

> Haskins, Ekaterina. "Between Archive and Participation: Public Memory in a Digital Age." *Rhetoric Society Quarterly*, 2007, pp. 401–422.

Abstract

In "Between Archive and Participation," Haskins argues that rhetoricians must consider the effects of new media on memory including the public obsession with memory and the "acceleration of amnesia."

Notes

Haskins says that the promises of digital media include multiple authorship, interactivity, diversity of content. She also says that there are lots of problems: self-congratulatory amnesia, participation shaped by commercial patterns of experience

insularity = characteristic of isolated people

active memory work vs. compulsive collection of traces

Quotes

"relegating the task of remembering to official institutions and artifacts arguably weakens the need for a political community actively to remember its past" (402).

"Associated with the rise of capitalism and the modern nation-state, these institutions of memory have tended to promulgate official ideologies of the ruling elites while claiming to speak on behalf of the people" (402).

"The glut of archival memory is a by-product of rapid obsolescence" (407).

"If archival preservation and retrieval are not balanced by mechanisms that stimulate participatory engagement, electronic memory may lead to self-congratulatory amnesia" (407).

Queries

What does Haskins mean by "relegating the task of remember?"

Connections

This essay reminds me of how everyone is always saying that the Internet is making people stupid because they can't focus on one thing very long. We're like goldfish swimming in a bowl. This essay also reminds me of these other things that I want to read.

Gillis, John R. "Memory and Identity: A History of a Relationship." Commemorations: The Politics of National Identity.

Huysen, Andreas. Twilight Memories: Marking Time in a Culture of Amnesia.

GETTING A GRADE

This assignment will be graded using a four-point scale based on the writing exercise rubric for undergraduate writing.

4 means the writing is well developed, original, and succeeds in mastering new techniques and knowledge. The writing shows risks that work.

3 means the writing has been done with considerable care and attention. It is developed and detailed.

2 means that the writing is acceptable. The student needs to spend more time or thought on the assignment

1 means that the writing is unacceptable. It maybe unfinished, inappropriate to the assignment, or written hastily.

0 means the student did not turn in any writing.

Exercise—Genre Analysis

Any time you are faced with a new writing situation, it is useful to find examples of the type of thing you are being asked to write. Once you find some examples, the next step is to analyze the examples to determine what your audience will be expecting. You also want to identify opportunities to be creative and try out new things.

Remember that to analyze something means to break it down into its parts.

Think about the following questions to help you analyze a document:

- What is the main purpose of the document?

- Is it clear whether you are looking at a stronger or more successful example? How can you tell?

- What are the parts of the document? Can you list them?

- How would you describe the author's tone? Choose three words that best describe how he or she sounds.

- If you had to produce the same type of document, what parts do you think you have to use? What parts do you think you could change?

Next, **write** a short paper (300–600) words in which you address the questions above and any other insights you gain through your analysis. Remember, a genre analysis of one type of document should aid you in making your own.

GETTING A GRADE

This assignment will be graded using a four-point scale based on the writing exercise rubric for undergraduate writing.

4 means the writing is well developed, original, and succeeds in mastering new techniques and knowledge. The writing shows risks that work.

3 means the writing has been done with considerable care and attention. It is developed and detailed.

2 means that the writing is acceptable. The student needs to spend more time or thought on the assignment

1 means that the writing is unacceptable. It maybe unfinished, inappropriate to the assignment, or written hastily.

0 means the student did not turn in any writing.

Exercise—Peer Response Letter

For this exercise, produce a one-page letter for a classmate that provides feedback on the person's writing project. For more information on collaboration, read "Collaborating" in *Easy Writer*.

GROUND RULES

- Format your response as a formal letter in order to practice the conventions of letter writing. If you aren't sure how to format a letter, then consult the Purdue OWL's useful online resource on business letters.

- Be amiable.

- Begin your letter by articulating what you think the author's main point is.

- Provide one paragraph describing strengths in the writing that you read.

- Provide one paragraph describing things you think the author could work on or questions you had as a reader.

- Use what you've learned in the course so far to provide meaningful and specific feedback.

- Write your letters as word documents and attach them to your e-mail responses. This will make them easier to find and use in your portfolios.

- Copy your instructor on all communication related to your peer response.

GETTING A GRADE

This assignment will be graded using a four-point scale based on the writing exercise rubric for undergraduate writing.

4 means the writing is well developed, original, and succeeds in mastering new techniques and knowledge. The writing shows risks that work.

3 means the writing has been done with considerable care and attention. It is developed and detailed.

2 means that the writing is acceptable. The student needs to spend more time or thought on the assignment

1 means that the writing is unacceptable. It maybe unfinished, inappropriate to the assignment, or written hastily.

0 means the student did not turn in any writing.

Exercise—Reflection Letter

On the first page of your assignment, before the text of your paper, please write a letter explaining what you were trying to do in this paper, what seemed to work, what didn't, how the paper developed and changed from invention through drafting to revision, the effectiveness of your response workshop, what major decisions you made in composing it, and what you learned from the assignment. Reflect on your process. Be sure to connect this work to your work in English 102 as a whole—be deliberate about how you see this piece as a component of your learning in relationship to the writing you have already done and will continue to do in class. Please also include specific details about what kind of feedback you want.

It may help you to consider the following questions:

- What worked in this assignment? What did you learn? What was challenging? What is important about how this work is evolving?

- How well do you think you did on this assignment? Analyze your work in terms of the rubric. Which rubric descriptors do you feel sure about? Which ones do you need to work on? Explain.

- How do you expect this work to feed your final portfolio? What did you learn from doing it that will affect the way you write future assignments or revise past ones?

- What specific feedback do you want from your instructor? What would you like your instructor to notice or respond to?

- What were your troublespots? How might this assignment be taught differently in the future to help students do better work?

- What help do you need? As you put the pieces together, what questions do you have? Are there any specific ideas, tasks, or lessons that should be addressed in class?

GETTING A GRADE

This is a credit/no credit assignment. You will not receive a grade, but you will receive full credit if you complete the assignment according to the guidelines.

APPENDIX B: POLISHING YOUR PAPER

This appendix features activities that you can use to polish just about any paper you've written.

Polishing Your Paper: Choosing the Right Word

On pages one through ten of your *Easy Writer* textbook, you'll find a list of the twenty most common errors first-year writers make in their writing. What is interesting is that by far the most common error for first-year writers is choosing the wrong word. As Andrea Lunsford suggests,

> twenty years ago, spelling errors were most common by a factor of more than three to one. The use of spell checkers has reduced the number of spelling errors in student writing—but spell checkers' suggestions may also be responsible for some (or many) of the wrong words students are using. (1)

That's because the spell checker will suggest a correctly spelled word that sounds like the word the writer is trying to use even though the spell check suggestion has a different meaning.

Here are a few words and phrases to watch out for:

- manner vs. manor
- for all intents and purposes vs. for all intensive purposes
- definitely vs. defiantly
- credible vs. creditable
- there vs. their vs. they're
- its vs. it's
- let's vs. lets
- then vs. than
- possess vs. posses
- manager vs. manger
- customer vs. costumer

Here's a two-step method for reducing and eliminating these mistakes in your writing.

Step 1: Read your paper out loud slowly. Reading slowly is important because the sound may help you identify things that are working and aren't working.

Step 2: Make a list. Write down any words or phrases that are not correct as well as their corrections. You can also write down any words that you want to double check, just to make sure you're using them correctly. Use this page to start your list.

Polishing Your Paper: Introductory Elements

The second most common mistake among first-year writers is a missing comma after introductory elements. An introductory element is "any word, phrase, or clause that precedes the subject of a sentence" (Lunsford 110). Here is an example:

To pass the course, students must attend class and spend time studying.

Here are a few words and phrases that might help you identify introductory elements:

Before	(Before going to class, you need to…)
After	(After I got home, I…)
However	(However, I feel that…)
Although	(Although the topic was boring, the speaker…)
As	(As time went by, I began to realize…)
On the other hand	(On the other hand, I like…)

Here are two strategies for identifying introductory elements in your writing.

Strategy #1: On the Computer. Use the search feature in your word processor to search for each of the phrases above. Read each example one-by-one and decide if you have an introductory element that needs a comma.

Strategy #2: On Paper. Scan your paper for each of these words and phrases. When you find one, highlight it. When you finish scanning for each, go back and decide whether or not you need to add a comma.

Just for fun, record all of the introductory elements you find in your paper on this page and count how many times you use each one. You might start to see a pattern, which will give you an opportunity to talk to your instructor about style and sentence variation.

For more on commas with introductory elements, see the section on commas in *Easy Writer.*

Polishing Your Paper: Insufficient Citation

The third most common mistake among first-year writers is insufficient citation. This means that writers will make reference to a source but forget to include an in-text citation or all of the information that is necessary for a reader. Here is an example:

> Andrea Lunsford explains that "source citations demonstrate that you've done your homework on your topic and that you are a part of a conversation surrounding it."

While the sentence above clearly contains a direct quote, it does not provide enough information to the reader about where the quote came from. Instead, the sentence should look like this:

> Andrea Lunsford explains that "source citations demonstrate that you've done your homework on your topic and that you are a part of a conversation surrounding it" (208).

The second sentence tells the reader not only that the quote came from Andrea Lunsford but also that the reader can find the quote on page 208 of the book.

Here are two strategies for identifying places that need sufficient citation in your writing.

Strategy #1: On the Computer. Use the word processor's highlight or underline feature to mark all passages that reference outside sources. This will give you a visual signal for identifying all of the spots that come from someone else. It is especially helpful if you find yourself copying quotes from other electronic sources directly into your writing. Remember that insufficient citation is linked to plagiarism concerns. Be thoughtful and careful when copying from other sources.

Strategy #2: On Paper. Write all of your quotes, paraphrases, and any other references to outside sources on 3×5 inch notecards and then tape or paste them onto a page of your writing wherever they will appear. This too will give you a visual signal for identifying all of the spots that come from someone else.

For more on using MLA documentation styles, see the section on integrating sources and avoiding plagiarism in *Easy Writer*.

Polishing Your Paper: Pronoun References

The fourth most common mistake among first-year writers has to do with pronoun references. This means that writers will use pronouns like *they* but do not clarify what exactly *they* refers to. Here is an example:

> The cup of coffee on the table spilled onto the computer after it wobbled.

It's not clear in the sentence above what actually did the wobbling. Was it the cup, the table, or the computer? Editing the sentence can help make sure the audience doesn't get confused.

> The cup of coffee on the table spilled onto the computer after the table wobbled.

Here are two strategies for identifying places that need clear pronoun references in your writing.

Strategy #1: On the Computer. Use the search feature in your word processor to search for pronouns like her, his, it, and their. Read each example one-by-one and decide if the pronoun has a clear antecedent—the noun or noun phrase that a pronoun replaces.

Strategy #2: On Paper. Scan your paper for pronouns like her, his, it, and their. When you find one, highlight it. When you finish scanning for each, read each example one-by-one and decide if the pronoun has a clear antecedent—the noun or noun phrase that a pronoun replaces.

For more on using pronouns, see the section on pronouns in *Easy Writer*.

APPENDIX C: ALTERNATIVE ARRANGEMENTS

In addition to the arrangement of this book, there are other ways your instructor may choose to organize your writing for the semester based on genres and rhetorical purposes.

Alternative Arrangement

This arrangement postpones the narrative project until students have fully investigated their course topics, which enables the narrative to be a story that integrates the students' research and learning.

Project 1: Profile Project

Project 2: Analysis Project

Project 3: Midterm Portfolio

Project 4: Exploratory Project

Project 5: Narrative Project

Project 6: Final Portfolio